VANISHED CITY

London's Lost Neighbourhoods

Tom Bolton

Chapter title page and colour section photography by SF Said.
All other photographs by Tom Bolton.

First Published by Strange Attractor Press 2014
Text Copyright © 2014 Strange Attractor Press / Tom Bolton
Photographs Copyright © 2014 SF Said
Design: Etienne Gilfillan

ISBN: 978-1907222290
A CIP catalogue record for this book is available from the British Library.

Strange Attractor Press
BM SAP, London, WC1N 3XX, UK
www.strangeattractor.co.uk

Printed in the UK

Contents

INTRODUCTION

"The true identity of London, he said, is in its absence. As a city it no longer exists. In this alone it is truly modern. London was the first metropolis to disappear."

London (dir. Patrick Keiller, 1994)

Every place consists of layers of accumulated and discarded past, visible and invisible, and London more so than most. In the City of London 2,000 years of building and destruction are capped with a thin skin of tarmac, paving slabs and the occasional cobble. Underneath the layers run 35 feet deep, and the Square Mile teeters on a heap of its own bricks and bones. London has cast off many skins. As its edges have advanced, what was once edge has become centre. Waves of change break across familiar places, burying and replacing the past without hesitation.

A definitive guide to lost London is an impossible task. Most of the time change comes stealthily, creeping behind our backs, failing to provide advanced notice or to mark full stops. Yet it is also impossible to consider living London without thinking about what used to be, and wondering how we have ended up with this particular place. Given London's capacity for reinvention it is no surprise that so many previous versions have been discarded and forgotten, yet the strangeness and difference hidden in apparently familiar locations continues to fascinate and feed the city.

London's absences are both too large to comprehend and too small to notice. Wartime bombing reshaped every part of the city, arbitrarily removing the familiar. The docks that gave East London its rationale left huge holes in their wake, now thinly papered over. While new streets rise conspicuously at King's Cross and the Heygate Estate vanishes for good in plain sight, other disregarded neighbourhoods disappear quietly with no crane-framed spectacle to attract attention.

At the same time the city is in constant motion and pieces of its fabric have a disconcerting habit of vanishing. Once out of sight, their memory fades and it requires a great effort of will to remember what filled a hole only days old. Disappearances are nominal as well as physical. Once well-known places names have drifted out of circulation. Bagnigge Wells, Garratt, Hatcham, Hockley-in-the-Hole, the Neat House Gardens, the Old Mint, the Old Nichol, Oxford Market and Thorney Island are a few of the entries in a lengthy reckoning of the vanished city. Meanwhile names remain a powerful commodity, and reassigned identities are all around. In Holborn tourist guides wear jackets declaring themselves in "Mid-Town", while around the Shard private security stakes out "The London Bridge Quarter". Naming rights are contested, and places shift and realign.

The ten forgotten neighbourhoods in this book are a few of the many lost Londons. Each of the places revived here were once very well-known to an average Londoner. Their locations still exist but have transformed into something entirely different, where the clues to past lives are easily overlooked. Some performed gradual vanishing acts over centuries – Horselydown, worn away by railway lines, warehouses, social change and redevelopment; Streatham Spa, fallen out of fashion; Wellclose, demolished with little regard for its remarkable past. Some vanished spectacularly – Cripplegate, burned to the ground in a Second World War firestorm – or shone briefly and gloriously, like White City. Limehouse Chinatown was a curious combination of East End history and a myth that transcended reality. Agar Town and Clare Market were deliberately scrubbed from the map by those who thought they disgraced the city. Norton Folgate and Ratcliff remain on the map but, superseded by larger neighbours, their names have fallen into disuse and their history is obscured.

London has been made and remade through destruction and renewal, but everything leaves traces. *Vanished City* returns to demolished streets to tell their stories. It is a guide for those who seek the old, the strange, the forgotten, the hidden and the lost.

CLARE MARKET AND OLD DRURY LANE: THE LOST ROOKERY

What remains of Clare Market is fragmented, but the spirit of its knotted alleys lingers behind the office anonymity of Kingsway and the Aldwych embassies.

Introduction

Although it was London's Anglo-Saxon market, Aldwych lacks the historical profile of the Cities of London and Westminster. In fact its name, absent for 1,000 years, was revived in the early 20th century to give authenticity to newly built streets. Until this piece of Edwardian rebranding, the neighbourhood was named after a tangle of old streets around Clare Market. The dead straight Kingsway boulevard and the planned curve of the Aldwych, conspicuous breaks in London's medieval street pattern, give the game away. These super-wide avenues and their imposing buildings were a final Imperial *grand projet*, a boulevard fit for a king lined with offices that look like public buildings.

The neighbourhood they replaced could not have been more different.

The streets of Clare Market, demolished for the Aldwych and Kingsway, were a neglected remnant, still filled at the very end of the 19th century with buildings that had escaped the Great Fire. Their demolition, as the new century dawned, marked the end of a piece of Old London that would have been recognisable to Elizabethans. Tantalising hints remain of a place that vanished on the threshold of living memory. Its shadow helps to explain a neighbourhood where grand façades conceal a tangle of small streets. What remains of Clare Market is fragmented, but the spirit of its knotted alleys lingers behind the office anonymity of Kingsway and the Aldwych embassies.

The Old Town

After the departure of the Romans London is thought to have lain abandoned for at least 200 years but by 604, when the first St. Paul's Church was endowed by the Saxon King Ethelbert, it was coming back to life as an Anglo-Saxon town. There were two main centres: Lundenburh, the Fort of London within the old Roman City walls, and Lundenwic, a trading centre in the vicinity of modern Aldwych. Lundenwic, only fully uncovered in the 1980s, saw trade from the 7th century with ships unloading goods at the Fleet River wharves nearby at Blackfriars. The original settlement may have been Danish, hence the church of St. Clement Danes. The name Lundenwic disappeared during the 9th century but the name Aldwych, meaning 'old town', marks the area of the Anglo-Saxon settleent.

The name Aldwych was brought back to life when the modern street was built, but it had been preserved for many centuries as Wych Street, one of the main streets demolished for the construction of Aldwych and Kingsway in the early 1900s. Drury Lane is thought to have once been the 'Via de Aldwych', but took its new name from Drury House where, in 1601, the Earls of Essex and Southampton met to plot, unsuccessfully, against Elizabeth I.

Drury House was one of several large houses built on what, during the 16th century, was open land separating the Cities of London and Westminster. Another, Clare House on St. Clement's Fields, gave its name to Clare Market. Drury House was Craven House, built for the Earl of Craven during the 17th century, a complex of buildings with a large garden. After his time it became a tavern called The Queen of Bohemia, named after his mistress, the Winter Queen. He had fallen for her while fighting for her husband, Frederick V, in the Thirty Years War. Craven was a flamboyant character, coming to London as a poor Yorkshireman and making his fortune as a soldier. He went into exile with Charles II, returning in triumph and, unlike many others of his status, stayed in London during the Great Plague of 1665. He also found time to annoy Samuel Pepys with his chairmanship of the Committee on Fisheries ("very confused and very ridiculous") and his military abilities ("riding up and down to give orders, like a madman").[1]

By the 17th century Drury Lane was still favoured by the powerful: Carolean aristocrats including the Earl of Anglesey and the Earl of Argyll, had houses there, while Oliver Cromwell lodged in Drury Lane during the Civil War. Houses began to fill the space between Lincoln's Inn and the Strand, and by 1700 Lincoln's Inn Fields was the only open area left. The square is thought to have been planned by Inigo Jones, although the story that its dimensions match those of the base of the Great Pyramid appears, unfortunately, not to be true.

Remarkably, one of the first buildings in the area survives: the Old Curiosity Shop on Portsmouth Street, built in 1567 in the reign of Elizabeth I. Somehow it is still there, entirely out of scale with its surroundings but protected by its starring role in Charles Dickens' novel of the same name.

The first building at Clare Market was put up in 1657 on St. Clement's Fields: "Towards Drury Lane, a new market, called Clare Market; then is there a street and palace of the same name, built by the Earl of Clare, who lived there in a princely mansion, having a house, a street, and a market both for flesh and fish, all bearing his name."[2] It was predominantly a meat market, with butchers' premises and slaughterhouses spreading into the surrounding streets and courtyards.

By 1720 the market was established and well-used, John Strype describing "a broad Place with Shambles and Stalls built, as designed for a market" (a shambles being a slaughterhouse). He added that Clare Market was "very considerable and well served with provisions, both flesh and fish; for, besides the butchers in the shambles, it is much resorted unto by the country butchers and higglers"[3] (higglers were street traders). The meat market remained popular for 150 years. However, by the early 1700s Clare Market and Drury Lane had already begun to go downhill. As London grew, courtyards and alleys full of poorly built housing sprang up and the nobility sold their houses and moved away to less crowded parts of town. In their place came the theatres.

The play

Drury Lane was known for its cockpits, which were also sometimes used as theatres, but after Charles II was restored to the throne in 1660 it became the centre of the revived London stage and a theatreland that still revolves around the same streets. Oliver Cromwell's Protectorate had banned the theatre as immoral, but the King and his brother, the Duke of York, granted licenses to two new theatre companies. Both began life in the ageing Cockpit Theatre on Drury Lane, but soon moved to real tennis courts, off Clare Market. These were long, galleried buildings, relatively easy to convert for performances.

The King's Company converted Gibbon's Tennis Court off Clare Market into the Vere Street Theatre in 1660. Their repertoire included female actors performing for the first time on the public stage. The first play with a woman in the cast is thought to have been *Othello*, staged in December 1660, with Desdemona played by an actress

Clare Market, at the junction with Portugal Street

called Margaret Hughes. The new theatre proved a sensation with a public starved of entertainment under Cromwell. Samuel Pepys watched a play called *Beggar's Bush* there and became quite carried away: "Here I saw the first time one Moone, who is said to be the best actor in the world, lately come over with the King, and indeed it is the finest play-house, I believe, that ever was in England."[4]

However, the novelty soon wore off and audiences moved on to the next new thing: the Lincoln's Inn Fields Theatre on Portugal Street, where the Duke's Company had converted Lisle's Tennis Court, opened in 1661, and was both larger and more sophisticated than Vere Street. It was the first theatre with moveable stage scenery, used in its opening production of an opera called *The Siege of Rhodes*. Charles II made his first visit to a theatre in order to see the show which also featured Thomas Betterton, soon to become the leading actor of his time.

The fierce competition continued as The King's Company left Vere Street for another new theatre in 1663. This was the King's Playhouse, Bridges Street, on the same site as the current Theatre Royal Drury Lane (which is the fourth incarnation of the theatre, after each of its three predecessors burned down). By the early 1700s the area was established as the centre of London theatre. The New Theatre, built in 1714 to replace the Lincoln's Inn Fields Theatre, staged John Gay's phenomenally successful *The Beggar's Opera*. It was produced by John Rich, and said to have made "Rich gay and Gay rich".

The Vere Street Theatre became slaughterhouses and carpenters' workshops, which burned down in 1809. However, there is now a theatre on the site again. After a gap of 200 years, one of the oldest theatrical locations in London was brought back into use by the impresario Oscar Hammerstein, who built the London Opera House on Kingsway at great expense. It opened in 1911 and closed all of eight months later

The chequered history of the site continued as it became the equally unsuccessful National Theatre of England; then a cinema. As the Stoll Theatre it specialised in musicals and ice shows, but closed with the landmark Stratford production of *Titus Andronicus*, starring Laurence Olivier and Vivien Leigh. The Stoll Theatre was demolished in 1957 and replaced by offices, with a theatre called the Royalty in the basement. The London School of Economics (LSE) bought it in the 1990s and renamed it the Peacock Theatre, and it now stages both lectures and dance.

The pleasures of the Lane

The opening of the King's Playhouse in 1663 brought famous actors to the Lane, including Nell Gwynne who lived there at the height of her fame. Samuel Pepys, on May Day 1667, "saw pretty Nelly standing at her lodgings' door in Drury-lane in her smock sleeves and bodice, looking upon one: she seemed a mighty pretty creature."[5]

Other late 17th century stage stars who lived in the vicinity included Barton Booth on Bow Street, Colley Cibber on Charles Street, and David Garrick on Southampton Street. The less well-known actors, however, lived in the Clare Market neighbourhood, lodging in its numerous courts, places such as Bear Yard, Craven Buildings and Vinegar Yard, near the theatres so that "we could all be mustered by beat of drum, could attend rehearsals without any inconvenience, and yet save coach-hire."[6]

The comic actor James Spiller was a working class hero, especially popular with the market butchers, who supposedly replaced the sign at the Bull and Butcher pub on Clare Market with one for 'The Spiller's Head'. When Spiller died in 1730, the butchers wrote a lament: "Down with your marrow-bones and cleavers all / And on your marrow-bones ye butchers fall / For prayers from you who never prayed before / Perhaps poor Jemmy may to life restore."[7]

Clare Market was at the centre of a web of confusing back streets, the grubby backstage to the Drury Lane footlights, with a reputation for the sort of pubs frequented by those who were hard up. Drury Lane was also a place where hack writers lodged, as Alexander Pope noted: "Cries he who high in Drury Lane / Lulled by soft zephyrs through the broken pane / Rhymes ere he wakes, and prints before Term ends / Obliged by hunger, and request of friends."[8] It was the neighbourhood of choice for those who scraped their living around the disreputable fringes of the arts, "the drabs and bloods of Drury Lane."[9]

Inevitably, the streets off Drury Lane gained a reputation for prostitution and serious drinking. Thomas Gay wrote "O may thy Virtue guard thee through the Roads / Of Drury's mazy Courts and dark Abodes!"[10] An account in the early 1700s claimed "There are reckoned to be one hundred and seven 'pleasure-houses' within and about this settlement; and a Roman Catholic priest, who has lodged here many years, assures me that to his knowledge the Societies for

Space House, Kingsway

the Reformation of Morals have taken as much pains, and expended as large sums to reclaim this new Sodom, as would have fitted out a force sufficient to have conquered the Spanish West Indies."[11]

In *The Tatler*, Richard Steele described a district divided into particular "ladyships," analogous to "lordships" in other parts, "over which matrons of known ability preside."

Drury Lane was the setting for William Hogarth's 'The Harlot's Progress', a sequence of paintings in which a country girl becomes a prostitute and ends up in the Bridewell Prison before dying of venereal disease. The Artists' Club, of which Hogarth was a member, used to meet at the Bull's Head Tavern in Clare Market.

The reputation of the district for entertainment goes back to the Strand maypole. A maypole was recorded in 1661 at Strand Cross, where St. Mary le Strand Church is today. It was 134 feet high and made of cedar, a replacement for a predecessor taken down by Oliver Cromwell's government in 1644. In 1713 a new pole with two gilt balls and a weather vane on top was put up, but by 1717 was already said to be rotten. It was taken down, and acquired by Sir Isaac Newton who had it re-erected in Wanstead Park to support the world's largest telescope. The maypole was lamented in verse by James Bramston, who wrote "What's not destroyed by Time's devouring hand? / Where's *Troy* and where's the *May-Pole* in the *Strand*?"[12]

The great clown Joseph Grimaldi was the archetypal back street stage star, who gravitated from the alleys to the Lane. He was born on Stanhope Street, at the heart of the Clare Market kasbah, in 1778. Grimaldi's father Giuseppe was an actor, a dancer and ballet master at the Theatre Royal. He was also a philanderer with at least ten children with three different women, and an eccentric obsessed with death. He would fake his own death in front of his children and, when he eventually died for real, he left a clause in his will giving his eldest daughter Mary five pounds if she would behead him to prevent his being buried alive.

Joseph Grimaldi, acclaimed as a stage genius, worked all his life at the Theatre Royal and the Covent Garden Theatre. He turned the low comedy role of the Clown into the starring role through his harlequinade performances, and was admired by Lord Byron. He was also, unexpectedly, a butterfly collector who had a cabinet with 4,000 specimens, including a Camberwell Beauty. Grimaldi died in 1837, brought down by alcoholism, debt, misfortune and poor health, said to be caused by the physical exertion of his performances. He gave his last performance at the Theatre Royal, Drury Lane.

Decline and fall

The decline of Clare Market accelerated in the 19th century, as the overcrowding multiplied and conditions in the alleys and courtyards became significantly worse. In 1850, the Bear Yard slaughterhouse was butchering 400 sheep and 60 bullocks every week, while the yard and alley housed the equally antisocial meat processing industries, including tripe boilers and tallow makers. Crowded housing and butchery made Clare Market somewhere to avoid.

The fetid atmosphere is illustrated by the macabre story of Enon Chapel.[13] In 1822 William Holmes built a dissenters' chapel a little north of today's St. Clement's Passage, where he served as the minister. He extended his duties to include the illicit burial of the dead under the chapel floor. He sold the burial clothes from the corpses, having boiled them clean, and burned the wood from their coffins in his hearth, leaving the bodies rotting in a basement vault.

The chapel closed in 1835, but it was not until 1844 that excavations for a new sewer led to the bodies being discovered – 12,000 of them. Remarkably, nothing was done even then, and the building was used for a further three years – as a prize-fighting ring, a casino, a concert room and a penny theatre – all on top of a pile of rotting corpses. This was gleefully advertised as "Enon Chapel – Dancing on the Dead – Admission Threepence. No lady or gentleman admitted unless wearing shoes and stockings".[14] It was only in 1848 that the bodies were disinterred and reburied at West Norwood Cemetery. This grim story gives a vivid sense of the general odour levels in the neighbourhood, which made it possible ignore a vast pit of putrefying corpses for the best part of 25 years.

Demolition began in the area in the first half of the 19th century. St. Clement Danes Church, now sitting on an island at the entrance to Fleet Street, was surrounded by narrow lanes. As John Gay put it, "Where the fair columns of Saint *Clement* stand / Whose straiten'd Bounds encroach upon the *Strand* / Where the low Penthouse bows the Walker's Head / And the rough Pavement wounds the yielding Tread."[15] Butcher's Row, known for its slaughterhouses, was a particularly striking street of wood and plaster houses, some dating from the reign of Henry VIII, overhanging the street at first floor level. This was one of the first streets to be demolished early in the 1800s, driven by a modernising horror of their "wretched fabrics, the receptacles of filth in every corner, the bane of old London, and a sort of nestling-place for the plague and fevers."[16] In 1868, 450 houses were demolished for the construction of the Royal Courts of Justice, on the edge of the slum area east of Clare Market, and a series of courts cleared including Bear and Harrow Court, Chair Court, Star Court and Swan Court.

The southern part of what is now Serle Street was also cleared. It had once been Sheer Lane, where the antiquary Elias Ashmole had lived and where the Kit Cat Club was founded. However, it had become far from respectable, and was renamed in an attempt to change its reputation. As Lower Serle's Place it had a reputation for crime, with stories about escape routes through the houses which were home to 'thieves' kitchens' or 'cadgers' halls'. A few hundred yards away, Newcastle Court "was one of the lowest haunts of this parish, and consisted entirely of houses of ill-fame of the worst description, stored with the foulest moral pollution." It was apparently characterised by "Abandoned women, old and young, decked in tawdry finery, bloated with gin and debauchery".[17]

In the 1870s the St. Clement Danes magazine reported "I have seen miseries of poverty and sickness in the Roman Ghetto, and in the plague quarter of Cairo; but there are places in the neighbourhood of Clare Market that would beat them hollow – very nightmares of poverty and disease."[18] Charles Dickens Junior wrote in 1879 that "Nowhere in London is a poorer population to be found than that which is contained in the quadrangle formed by the Strand, Catherine-street, Long-acre, and Lincoln's-inn and the new law courts."[19] However, there were attempts to improve the neighbourhood. King's College Hospital opened on Clare Market in 1840 to train medical students, and became popular and well-known. Joseph Lister pioneered antiseptics for surgery there in 1877. The hospital moved out to its current site at Denmark Hill in 1909, as the population began to shift away from the crowded central London slums of which Clare Market was typical. The hospital building was replaced by the block that now contains the LSE Library, but the Royal College of Surgeons remains next door on Lincoln's Inn Fields, on the site of the New Theatre.

Past glories

By the second half of the 19th century there was a rising tide of protest at the state of the area. Novelist Mrs. Henry Wood, writing in 1869, talked of "those awful places round Drury Lane where thieves and cutthroats live."[20] *The Builder* claimed jokily that "The whole nest of streets and passages behind the south side of Lincoln's Inn Fields requires re-arrangement and improvement. There is a legend hereabout that years ago a young man from the country, bearing a black bag, started one winter night from Portugal Street to get into the Strand, and that he has been wandering round and about ever since, constantly returning with a disconsolate aspect to his original starting-point. On foggy nights his form may be descried in Clare Market."[21]

In 1880 it was still possible for J. Ewing Ritchie to claim that the majority of Londoners working in London lived "in Whitechapel, in Westminster and in Drury Lane."[22] Ritchie, a sensationalist writer with an agenda, saw what he wanted to see in Drury Lane. Although overcrowding and problems with drinking were indisputable, he claimed that people lived in overcrowded conditions by choice, despite working miles away. One man, he asserted, lived in Clare Market but worked in Aldershot. His belief that the place and the people were locked in a cycle of immorality and poverty was typical of many commentators of the time, and fed the belief that Clare Market, Drury Lane and the maze of back courts and alleyways were rotten, and had to be destroyed: "It has ever been a spot to be shunned", [23] wrote Richie.

George Gissing describes matter-of-factly in 1891 "…turning out of Leicester Square into the slum that leads to Clare Market".[24] Charles Booth's poverty survey of 1898 classifies much of the area on the west side of Clare Market, bounded by Great Queen Street, Drury Lane, The Strand, and Lincoln's Inn Fields as 'very poor' or 'vicious, semi-criminal'. Booth toured the neighbourhood after some of the Drury Lane courts had already been demolished, and people he met in the street implored him, assuming he was an official, "Don't pull our houses down guv'nor, before building us up others to go into."[25]

Booth claimed that the area was becoming worse as demolition advanced along Drury Lane, displacing residents into the nearest, cheapest accommodation. The north end of the Lane receives a particularly grim report, "a noticeable absence of happiness in these streets." Clare Market and surrounding streets are a mixed, working class neighbourhood, with some particularly poor streets with casual wards for the homeless and lodging houses for men. The area is summed up by Booth's detached observation on Goldsmith Street of "faces at windows of criminal type, but windows themselves fairly clean."

By this time the butchers had gone from Clare Market, but the market was in business although down on its luck, selling haddock, kippers and bread. The policeman accompanying Booth alleged that the inhabitants of nearby White Horse Yard "would not be past dropping a brick on my head if they got the chance." Booth describes "very dirty children on the pavement in groups" in Kemble Street; on Little Wild Street "the buildings do not look so bad, but… the smell inside is awful". Flower girls arrange bunches of roses for Covent Garden Market on the pavements. Holywell Street, more of a thoroughfare, is very busy with "second class booksellers and chemists of doubtful reputation". Booth describes "many small public houses, full today of women and children" but "no opium dens", which put it in a class above parts of the East End. At least no foreign sailors lived there.

London School of Economics Old Building, Houghton Street

A new Broadway

Plans to fill a notable gap in the central London road network, by linking Holborn to the Strand, were first drawn up as early as 1836. Southampton Row ran halfway towards the Strand from Euston Road, through the Duke of Bedford's land, but stopped at the estate boundary. The remaining half mile south of High Holborn was full of the small, winding streets of Clare Market and Drury Lane, with no direct route to the Thames. Plans came and went through the 19th century. A scheme from 1847 was designed to improve access with a new street leading to the new Public Records Office on Chancery Lane while another scheme for a through road fell through in 1883.

Plans for a new road were linked to the widening of the Strand, which narrowed between St. Mary le Strand and St. Clement Danes churches and was targeted for improvement. In 1892 a widening scheme involved building a new headquarters for the London County Council (LCC) and renaming the Strand 'Council Broadway'. Another proposal involved a new City Hall south of Great Queen Street, and an ultra-modern, multi-storied street all the way to Elephant and Castle with its own Thames bridge. It was to have railway lines below the surface, delivering passengers and goods directly into buildings.

Clare Market was living on borrowed time. Central London was becoming more commercialised and less residential, and the population of Holborn dropped by a third between 1871 and 1901. Finally the Improvement Act of 1897 put plans into action. By this time, the Strand widening plan and the new road from Southampton Way had been combined into a single project, along with "a scheme dealing with the insanitary areas in the neighbourhood of Clare Market", using the Housing of the Working Classes Act 1885 which made it easier to clear away 'unhealthy' housing.

Wrecking ball

Demolition began in 1899. Preparations involved erecting the largest hoarding ever seen in London, boarding up the Strand where Kingsway would be built. Photographs show hoardings three stories high, every inch neatly covered in advertisements for Allsopp's Pale Ale, Sandow's Embrocation and Mellor's Sauce (served by a butler, twice life-size).

By 1903 there were complaints that the work was taking too long, with much of the area empty and half of the parishes of both St. Clements and St. Mary le Strand demolished. The work was finally completed in 1905, entirely reshaping the neighbourhood and eliminating 28 acres of alleys and courts around Clare Market. Several well-known streets disappeared from the map, including Holywell Street, Little Queen Street, Newcastle Street, Stanhope Street, Vere Street and Wych Street. Three thousand people were displaced, more than half of whom were moved to the newly built Bourne Estate, on Clerkenwell Road.

Buildings demolished included the Sardinian Embassy Chapel on Kemble Street, which had at one time been London's unofficial Roman Catholic cathedral. It had been a target for anti-Catholic rioters, attacked when James II fled in 1688 and again in the Gordon Riots in 1780. The church of St. Anselm and St. Cecilia on Kingsway was built to replace it. Holy Trinity Church, Little Queen Street survived, but had to be knocked down in 1909 after it was undermined by excavations for the Piccadilly Line.

Also demolished was the entrance to Lincoln's Inn Fields from Sardinia Street through a strange, keyhole shaped archway under two 17th century houses. One was the Sardinian Ambassador's House, linked to a private pew in the Sardinian Embassy Chapel via a direct passageway. A companion keyhole arch on Remnant Street, given its name after being cut in half by Kingsway, survived until 1912.

Other buildings demolished included the Gaiety Theatre on Catherine Street, the Globe Theatre, the Opera Comique and the Olympic Theatre, on the former site of Drury House on Wych Street. One of the Inns of Court, New Inn next to the Royal Courts of Justice, was demolished. However, its neighbour Clement's Inn survived until just before the Second World War. This was where Shakespeare's Justice Shallow spent his allegedly wild student days – "I was of Clement's once myself, where they talk of Mad Shallow still" – and where he and Sir John Falstaff "heard the chimes at midnight".[26] Its buildings, which had been reconstructed in the 19th century, were demolished in 1934 but the alleyway between the Royal Courts of Justice and LSE is still called Clement's Inn.

The end of Wych Street

Wych Street was said to be the most picturesque street in London. After its demise it even inspired a popular short story called 'Where

Was Wych Street?' published in 1922. Back in 1889 *The Pall Mall Gazette* wrote "There still remain some picturesque old patchwork buildings in and around Wych Street, Holywell Street and Drury Lane. Their picturesqueness largely relies on the varied and uncertain angles of tottering timbers, and the promiscuous arrangement of windows which protrude and overhang the little shops… groaning under the mingled weight of years and heavy tread."[27]

Photographs taken during the summer of 1906 freeze the Clare Market neighbourhood in time, shortly before its final demolition. They show Wych Street looking more Elizabethan than Edwardian, the upper storeys of a row of plastered 17th century buildings overhanging the street. The Rising Sun, at the junction with Holywell Street, is a surviving Tudor tavern. The Shakespeare's Head on Wych Street, with huge glass lantern and a bust of the playwright over the door, looks just as old.

The photographs show Drury Lane half demolished, people still living in the remaining houses despite broken windows. Clare Market itself is mostly derelict. In nearby Denham Court a whitewashed cottage is the last building standing, a white 'X' painted on its front door, looking as though it belongs in the west of Ireland. In the background, the tower of St. Mary le Strand looms out of the mist.

One of the photographs shows a white-bearded and aproned man, standing alone in the doorway of his shop on Houghton Street, bowler hats on display in his window and a sign reading 'Gentlemen's Hats Polished for Sixpence'. The hat maker is caught full in the summer sun, eyes screwed up, the brightest object in the shadowy lane.

The new London

In the place of the old streets was Kingsway: three quarters of a mile long, 100 feet wide and dead straight providing, along with the Aldwych crescent, a formal setting for new, imperial-scale buildings. Edward Elgar even composed a song for the opening ceremony, with words by his wife ("The newest street in London town / Who'll pace it up and pace it down?"), perhaps not his greatest work.

The LCC deliberately chose one-word names for its new roads, to give them the weight of streets such as Cheapside, Piccadilly and Whitehall. Kingsway was named after the new King, Edward VII, and the association with the original Danish settlement at Aldwych was thought to be appropriate because of his Danish wife, Queen Alexandra.

The project was a symbol of the new London government introduced in 1889. The LCC was run until 1907 by the Progressive Party, an alliance of Liberal and Labour politicians, who engaged in a series of public improvement works beginning with the symbolic clearance of the notorious Old Nichol slum in Shoreditch. They moved people out of crowded inner city housing into new cottage developments in the suburbs, served by trams and rail.

The plans also owed a great deal to Baron Haussmann, even "to such an extent that it became the kind of location an impoverished film crew might choose to make a Maigret film without going to Paris."[28] Haussmann replanned Paris in the 1860s, replacing narrow, easily barricaded streets with wide boulevards which provided modern sewers and water mains, along with streets that were much harder to barricade. The building of the Aldwych and Kingsway has been described as 'the Haussmannisation of London', but in somewhat typical fashion for London the project took places decades after the Parisian version and consisted of a single pair of streets, hardly enough to reshape a city. London, perhaps fortunately, has never been much good at large-scale planning.

Kingsway makes more sense as a final piece of showmanship advertising an empire that was about to fall apart. It was paid for by increased land values rather than the public purse, so was not the piece of grand largesse it seemed. However, it took some years for it to become a commercial success and in 1914 still only half the Aldwych

St. Clement's Lane, off Sheffield Street

had been built up, and sites remained empty on Kingsway. It was finished only in 1922.

Boulevard of dreams

The Aldwych and Kingsway are continental-style streets, a little sterile and out of place in London which relies for its character on a less planned layout. The streets are lined with grey stone office edifices, including Adastral, Africa, Alexandra, Imperial, Ingersoll, Kodak, Princes, Regent, Victory, Windsor and York Houses. Adastral House, on the corner with the Aldwych, was the headquarters of the Air Ministry from 1918, also where the Met Office took its temperature measurements. It then became Television House, home of ITN, Associated-Rediffusion, Thames Television and London Weekend Television.

Aldwych was reserved for embassies, theatres and hotels. Both Australia and India Houses serve their original functions, as does the Waldorf Hilton. The Gaiety Theatre was demolished, replaced by the ME Hotel, but the Aldwych Theatre and the much renamed Novello Theatre (previously the Waldorf, the Strand, the Whitney and then the Strand again) are still operating. The BBC World Service left Bush House, the centrepiece of the entire scheme, in 2012 having first moved there during the Blitz in 1941.

Kingsway was an attempt to create a prototype street of the future but, as the only one of its kind, it became more of a curiosity. It operated at three levels, with Britain's only underground tram ('diver trams') running under the full length of the street from Holborn to Aldwych, and the Aldwych branch of the Piccadilly Line even further below. Part of the tram tunnel is now used by cars while the rest is disused, the entrance still clearly visible in the middle of Southampton Way.

The northern end of Kingsway is also home to a huge deep level bomb shelter, which was converted by the Post Office after the Second World War into a secret international telephone exchange, designed to carry on operating under future enemy attack. Its existence was exposed in 1980 by investigative journalist Duncan Campbell, by which time it had been decommissioned. It was put up for sale in 1996 although it is not clear who, if anyone, bought it.

21st century Clare Market

Remarkably enough, Clare Market itself remains on the map, now enveloped by a university campus. The London School of Economics was founded by four members of the Fabian Society, George Bernard Shaw, Graham Wallas, and Beatrice and Sidney Webb, in 1895. The site on Clare Market was acquired in 1902 from the LCC for a peppercorn rent, presumably helped by the fact that it was on the edge of the no-man's land cleared for Aldwych and Kingsway. The

Old Building was constructed as the first permanent home for the
School, and the LSE established itself, expanding into neighbouring
buildings as the need arose.

There is little doubt that 21st century Clare Market belongs to the
LSE, which has carved itself out an eccentric warren of courtyards,
back-streets and unexpected bridges and accumulated most of the
buildings between Aldwych, Kingsway and Lincoln's Inn Fields over
the course of half a century. Signs of resistance, such as the Ye Olde
White Horse pub on St. Clement's Lane which for years displayed a
'No Students' sign on its door, have faded away.

The LSE, by expanding gradually rather than engaging in major
demolition, has retained some of the feel of the Clare Market courts.
It remains a notoriously difficult place to navigate. Despite strenuous
efforts to scrub it from the map, the Clare Market slum has never
been completely rubbed out. Ducking off Kingsway, the atmosphere
changes and it is possible to understand how this could be one of
London's ancient centres.

REFERENCES

1   Pepys, Samuel, *The Diary of Samuel Pepys* Vol. 5 1664 University of California Press 2000

2   Howell, James, *Londinopolis: an historical discourse*, Twiford 1657

3   Strype, John, *A Survey of the Cities of London and Westminster*, 1720

4   Pepys, Samuel, *The Diary of Samuel Pepys* Vol. 1 1660 University of California Press 2000

5   Pepys, Samuel, *The Diary of Samuel Pepys* Vol. 8 1667 University of California Press 2000

6   Cook, William, *Memoirs of Charles Macklin, Comedian*, James Asperne 1804

7   Thornbury, Walter, *Old and New London: Volume 3*, Cassell 1879

8   Pope, Alexander, *Collected Poems*, J.M. Dent 1989

9   Goldsmith, Oliver, 'An Author's Bedchamber' *Everyman Poetry Library No. 30*, J.M.
     Dent 1997

10   Gay, John, *Selected Poems*, Fyfield Books 2003

11   Anon. *A View of London and Westminster: or, The Town Spy*, T. Warner 1728

12   Rogers, Pat, 'The Maypole in the Strand: Pope and the Politics of Revelry', *Journal for Eighteenth-Century Studies*, Vol. 28, Issue 1, pages 83–95, March 2005

13   Kiloh, George, *A History of LSE's Buildings*, LSE 2008

14   Fenn, Colin, 'The Cost of Burial at Norwood', *Friends of West Norwood Cemetery Newsletter*, No. 68, May 2010

15   Gay, John, *Selected Poems*, Fyfield Books 2003

16   Thornbury, Walter, *Old and New London: Volume 3*, Cassell 1879

17   Gordon, Charles, *Old Time Aldwych Kingsway and Neighbourhood*, T. Fisher Unwin 1903

18   Diprose, John, *Some account of the parish of St Clement Danes*, Diprose and Bateman, Vol 1 1868, Vol 2 1876

19   Dickens, Charles (the Younger), *Dickens' Dictionary of London*, 1888 http://www.victorianlondon.org/publications/dictionary.htm

20   Wood, Mrs Henry, *Roland Yorke*, Richard Bentley 1869

21   Thornbury, Walter, *Old and New London: Volume 3*, Cassell 1879

22   Ritchie, J. Ewing, *Days and Nights in London*, Tinsley 1880

23   *ibid*

24   Gissing, George, *New Grub Street*, Oxford University Press 1993

25   Booth, Charles, *Survey Into Life and Labour in London 1886-1903*, LSE Charles Booth Online Archive

26   Shakespeare, William, *Henry IV Part 2*, Arden Shakespeare 1967

27   *Pall Mall Gazette*, 17th October 1889

28   Hubert D. & Sutcliffe, J. 'The 'Haussmannisation' of London?: The Planning and Construction of Kingsway-Aldwych 1889-1935', *Planning Perspectives*, Vol. 11, No.2, April 1996, E&FN Spon

CRIPPLEGATE: THE FIERY CITY

The ancient, once familiar London district of Cripplegate vanished, literally overnight, in 1940.

Introduction

The Vanished City is neatly summed up by a story, probably apocryphal, about a cabbie. Black cab drivers are now known to have specially developed brains, expanded to memorise hundreds of London 'runs'. In short, the names and locations a cabbie does not know cannot be contained even by a specially adapted human brain. The cabbie in question, fully equipped with The Knowledge, was hailed by an elderly clergyman who asked to be taken to Cripplegate.[1] Try as he might, the driver could not place Cripplegate on his mental map. The passenger must have been elderly indeed because the ancient, once familiar London district vanished, literally overnight, in 1940. The name survives in stray incarnations, attached to a church and a City ward, but is essentially forgotten.

Second World War bombing caused enormous damage to London, but only at Cripplegate was an entire district erased. On the night of Sunday 29th December 1940, incendiary bombs ignited a firestorm which completely destroyed the area between Aldersgate and Moorgate, known since Saxon times as Cripplegate. Its eventual replacement, the Barbican, was so entirely different as to erase Cripplegate from memory as well as reality, but the towers and the highwalks cover a history as complex and peculiar as any London has to offer. The Barbican maze echoes the narrow, mysterious streets that came before, creating a place that, like its predecessor, seems to exist separately from the City. Cripplegate was a place of retreat, a combustible neighbourhood just beyond the City limits, so perhaps it is still present in spirit.

The gates to the City

Among London place names, Cripplegate has a uniquely medieval ring. An explanatory legend claims that the body of St. Edmund, the martyr king of East Anglia, miraculously cured cripples begging at the gate as it passed through. The story stuck and the new church, built just outside the gate in the City wall, was dedicated to St. Giles, the patron saint of the crippled.

However, the City gates go back to Roman London. The Roman city was surrounded by a solid stone wall, much of which still exists in basements, corners and back yards. It eventually had six gates which were, clockwise from the west, Ludgate (the road to the south-west), Newgate (the road to Silchester), Aldersgate, Cripplegate, Bishopsgate (Ermine Street, the road to York) and Aldgate (the road to Colchester). London Bridge linked the City to the Canterbury road. Later Moorgate was added.

The main City gates were purpose-built, defensible entrance ways, wide enough for carts and other traffic. Most were fortified buildings with upper stories and gates that could be slammed firmly

St. Giles Cripplegate and Lauderdale Tower

shut. However, there were also other, smaller gateways in the walls just for pedestrians. Cripplegate was located on Wood Street, just north of where it crosses London Wall today. It was unlike the other gates, originally built to access the Cripplegate fort where the Roman garrison was barracked, which was built into the City wall.

This fort was a 'barbican', meaning a defensive stronghold that was part of a wall. Its remains were discovered in 1949 at the corner of what is now Beech Street and Golden Lane, when the scale of wartime destruction gave archaeologists unprecedented access. It covered the area between St. Giles Church and Fann Street to the north of the Barbican, and was probably built in the early 2nd century AD under Emperors Trajan or Hadrian as the barracks for London, housing the Governor of Britain's personal guard of a thousand men.

Cripplegate Without

The Roman gates remained the main entrance points to the City long after the Roman era, and the City shrank back within its Roman shell. By the medieval era Cripplegate had become one of the main entrances to London. The longest remaining section of City wall survives, deep within the Barbican Estate. It was repaired in 1477 as part of works ordered by Sir Ralph Jocelyn, Mayor of London, on the wall between Aldersgate and Aldgate, using clay from the Moorfields nearby.

By the mid-1400s London had begun to grow again and villages formed outside the Roman walls. As the City spilled beyond the Roman limits areas that were inside, such as Cripplegate Within, developed equivalents outside, such as Cripplegate Without. Expansion beyond the walls meant space for industry. Cripplegate had workshops used by craftsmen specialising, like neighbouring Farringdon Without, in tannery and leatherwork. Another speciality was the archery suppliers of Grub Street where, in the 1590s, John Stow complained that that the popularity of guns was putting the bowyers, fletchers and bowstring makers out of business.

Medieval Farringdon Without soon became bigger than the whole of the City within the walls. Cripplegate, although smaller, spread along Grub Street (now Milton Street) and Whitecross Street and across the fields to Clerkenwell. Whitecross Street is thought to have taken its name from a white painted stone cross, outside the Holy Trinity Priory. Its lost companion, Redcross Street, derived its name from a cross that stood near the junction with Golden Lane, but is now Beech Street tunnel.

The Cripplegate itself was demolished in 1760 for road widening, but illustrations show that it was a substantial structure with a number of first floor rooms, which were used at various times as a prison and as a private house. Terry Farrell's vast post-modern Alban Gate office block on London Wall straddles the site and maintains the feeling of entering a fortified citadel.

The ghetto

Jews were encouraged to come to England by William the Conqueror, and in London they settled around the area of the City now marked by the streets called Old Jewry, off Cheapside, and in adjacent Cripplegate. This has been described by some sources as a ghetto, although this may mean that Jews chose to live here rather than they were obliged to do so. However, waves of anti-Semitic persecution were instigated by various monarchs until Edward I eventually expelled all Jews from England in 1290. Under King Stephen they had already been forbidden from burying the dead anywhere except in the Jews' Garden, which is thought to have been in Cripplegate on what later became known as Jewin Street (now beneath Defoe House on the Barbican Estate). This implies that the Jewish quarter occupied the area between Old Jewry and Cripplegate; Jewry Street, however, is at the eastern edge of the City, so Jewish London was probably more diverse than a single quarter or ghetto.

The Jewish population of Cripplegate may have vanished, but the area that developed outside the walls continued to house those on the margins. Its legacy of disreputable activity begins with the Fortune Theatre, built by impresario Philip Henslowe in 1600, previously responsible for the Rose Theatre on Bankside. Its site, conveniently located just beyond both the City's walls and its jurisdiction, is marked by a plaque on Fortune Street. After Henslowe's death, the Fortune was taken on by Edward Alleyn who at the same time was working to establish Dulwich College. When the English Civil War came, Parliament closed the theatres and in 1649 soldiers destroyed the interior of the Fortune. Dulwich College sold the remains for scrap.

Although William Shakespeare did not work at the Fortune, he lodged close by on the other side of Cripplegate. It was a cheap neighbourhood, the choice of actors working in the theatre land north of the walls, from Cripplegate to Shoreditch. He lived on Silver Street, home to medieval London's silversmiths. Before the Reformation, the Church of St. Olave Silver Street had possessed a figure of Christ wearing silver shoes.

Shakespeare moved in with the French Huguenot Mountjoy family in the early 1600s and is thought to have written plays including *King Lear, Macbeth* and *Othello* while lodging with them. Christopher Mountjoy was a wig-maker, with a daughter called Mary. Mountjoy was disappointed that Stephen Bellott, his apprentice for six years, had left without proposing marriage to Mary. Mrs. Mountjoy asked Shakespeare to convince the two that they belonged together, which he did. We know this because in 1604 Shakespeare told the story in court, called as a witness after a quarrel in which Bellott sued Mountjoy for refusing to pay a dowry. This fragment of a story ends here, as there is no record of a court judgement. However, it is clear that Shakespeare was close to the Mountjoys.

The Mountjoys' house, on the corner of Silver Street and Monkwell Street, burned down in the Great Fire. It was replaced by the Cooper's Arms pub, well-known until it was destroyed during the Second World War. The site is now under a large block of City offices on Wood Street, just north of the graveyard that belonged to the vanished church of St. Mary Staining. A block in the Barbican Estate is, however, named Mountjoy House.

Dissent

The reputation of Cripplegate Without as a home for people who did not fit elsewhere grew during the 17th century. An early example was the famed recluse Henry Welby. A landowner from Lincolnshire, he shut himself away in a house on Grub Street for 44 years, until his death in 1636 at the age of 84. Supposedly he had never recovered from the shock he received when his younger brother tried to shoot him. Despite the fact that as a recluse his life was by definition uneventful, the playwright Thomas Heywood wrote his biography. Although he was never seen in public artists also cashed in and engravings of him with a long beard, looking depressed, were still being produced in the 1790s.

During the 17th century Cripplegate became associated with dissenting religion and politics. John Foxe, author of the *Book of Martyrs* and inspiration to later Puritans, was buried in St. Giles, Cripplegate and Oliver Cromwell was married there in 1620.

By the Civil War Cripplegate had developed a reputation as an enclave of radical Puritanism, with sects such as the Seventh Day Baptists setting up meeting houses. John Goodwin, a radical preacher based at St. Stephen's Coleman Street, supported the execution of Charles I and helpfully offered to pray with the King in his cell on the night of his death. Charles politely refused. After the deed was done the Calf's Head Club, based in an alley off Moorfields, caused a scandal by celebrating the anniversary of Charles' execution with a meal of symbolic dishes and the ritual burning of a calf's head, in place of the King. They finally stopped meeting in 1734, after an attack from an angry pro-Stuart mob.

In 1661, soon after the Restoration, a cooper called Thomas Venner led an impromptu rebellion from a room above a tavern in Coleman Street. He persuaded his congregation of Fifth Monarchists to bring the New Kingdom of Christ on earth into being by rushing into the streets of the City and slaying the followers of Baal. Fifty rebels broke into St. Paul's Cathedral and for four days fought detachments of troops around Threadneedle Street and Wood Street. They made a final stand in the Blue Anchor on Coleman Street, where 20 people were killed. Venner was executed, with many of his followers, on gallows set up in Redcross and Whitecross Streets. In the 18th century there was still a reminder of extreme Puritan days, an alley called Anabaptist Court off Redcross Street, and in 1870 there were still eight non-conformist chapels in the ward.

John Milton, who had lived nearby, was buried in St. Giles Cripplegate. His body was exhumed 100 years later in 1790, during

Bunhill Fields burial ground

repairs to the church. The workmen removed hair and teeth as
souvenirs, and the gravedigger exhibited the skeleton in its coffin,
charging visitors sixpence. The horrified poet William Cowper wrote
an article called 'On the late indecent liberties taken with the Remains
of Milton' and a statue was commissioned for the church as some sort
of recompense. Photographs of the shell of St. Giles, taken in 1940,
show Milton overturned among the bombed rubble.

Around 1700 Dr. Williams' Library for the use of non-conformist
ministers was set up on Redcross Street. A Welsh Presbyterian
bequeathed his collection of books and manuscripts and money to
house them in what sounds like a lost museum of curiosities featuring,
among other exhibits, an Egyptian mummy and a glass basin which
had held the water used to baptise Elizabeth I.

Dissenting Cripplegate can be examined at the Bunhill Fields burial ground, laid out for non-conformists in 1665. Here William Blake, John Bunyan and Daniel Defoe are all buried, creating a place of unparalleled attraction for those trying to locate London's soul on the A-Z. Iain Sinclair says of Bunhill Fields, "Everything I believe in, everything London can do to you, starts there. The theatre of obelisks and pyramids, of signs, symbols, prompts, whispers. The lovely lies that take you out into the night. That bless each and every pilgrimage".[2]

Grub Street

The part of Cripplegate within the old City walls was inhabited by people of influence, from Sir Thomas More, born on Milk Street, to Judge Jeffreys who lived on Aldermanbury. However, the Cripplegate neighbourhood outside the walls was attractive to outsiders of all kinds, not only those of religious persuasion. It was known for petty crime, forgery, and fortune-telling. Supposedly "the wizard and witch loved the spot, because it was convenient ground to receive visits from clients or customers."[3] In 1713 notorious thief-taker and master-criminal Jonathan Wild set up his headquarters next to St. Giles Church, where he managed a combination of thieves, prostitutes and stolen goods.

Grub Street, changed to the more respectable Milton Street in 1830, supposedly derived its name from the ditch beside the road, full of rubbish and maggots. The term entered the language, coined by 17th century poet Andrew Marvell, as a collective description for hack writers, a group as disreputable as any other inhabitants of Cripplegate. Dr. Johnson, in his *Dictionary*, defines Grub Street as "the name of a street in London much inhabited by writers of small histories, dictionaries, and temporary poems; whence any mean production is called Grub Street."[4] His dictionary entry also hails Grub Street as his home territory, ironically quoting Ulysses' cry of "Hail Ithaca!" on his return to his homeland.

Grub Street was a "mere stone's throw from the City within the walls: but in sociological terms it was light-years distant."[5] The street was described by John Strype as "indifferent, as to its Houses and Inhabitants; and sufficiently pestered with Courts and Alleys."[6] It was noisy, squalid, crowded and equipped with cheap, unpleasant lodgings. These were taken up in the 1700s by writers who often operated on the edge of the law, propagating slander for a small fee. It was also home to "pamphleteers, plagiarists, pornographers, balladists, dealers in dying confessions and… translators and proof readers housed in common beds above the farthing pie shops."[7] Some lodgings, apparently, housed hacks three to a bed, reflecting the pittance they were paid.

Grub Street was also the home of the earliest newspapers, including *The Daily Courant*, the first daily paper in England, which was founded in 1702. Daniel Defoe, who was born on Fore Street, operated in its dubious milieu. He worked on *Mist's Weekly Journal* as an agent for the Whig government, aiming to undermine its anti-government line. Meanwhile another journal, *The North Briton,* was set up by radical John Wilkes as a vehicle to attack the then Prime Minister, The Earl of Bute.

The booksellers of the 18th century were also publishers, who paid their writers as little possible. The power held by a small number of people fuelled the spectacular Grub Street feuds fought in the literature of the early 1700s. Alexander Pope's publisher, Edmund Curll, made his money as a purveyor of pornography, patent medicines, stolen letters, and as a pioneer of 'kiss-n-tell' publishing. After Curll printed poems against his instructions, Pope conducted a 20-year campaign against him. At four feet six inches tall he was too small to fight Curll, so instead Pope slipped an emetic into his drink and then issued a pamphlet claiming he was dead.

Pope, despite his diminutive stature, was more than able to stand up for himself. He set up *The Grub Street Journal* to attack poets and publishers he despised, and famously wrote *The Dunciad*, a mock heroic poem attacking the main characters of Grub Street. Curll features heavily, alongside actor and dramatist Colley Cibber and publisher Lewis Theobald, who are the Kings of the Dunces in the service of the goddess "Dulness". Curll defeats them both in a pissing contest. Grub Street is described as the "home of duncehood" where "While pensive poets painful vigil keep / Sleepless themselves, to give their readers sleep." Becoming the victim of the most entertaining and vindictive attack in the English language left Curll unfazed, and he not only commissioned ripostes such as *The Popiad*, but also made money from printing pirate editions of *The Dunciad* itself.

In other words, 18th century Cripplegate was lorded over by a shameless, warring family of hacks, too clever for their own good, whose quarrels were inseparable from their work. As a Grub Street poet called Ned Ward wrote in 1781: "O bury not my peaceful corpse / In Cripplegate, where discord dwells / And wrangling parties jangle worse / Than alley's scolds or Sunday's bell."[8]

The social status of writers was improving by the start of the 19th century and Grub Street lost its significance, but the phrase retained its power. When George Gissing wrote about the grim lives of low paid writers in late 19th century London, he called his novel *New Grub Street*.

Cripplegate trades

Eighteenth century Cripplegate was not, however, inhabited solely by writers. Small trades characterised the area from its medieval origins until the Second World War. In the mid-1700s Redcross and Whitecross Streets were the main thoroughfares of the neighbourhood, and the latter was "noble, wide, and well built, inhabited by persons of property."[9] Small trades dominated Cripplegate, in particular the 'rag trade'. Barbican was "a good broad Street, well inhabited by Tradesmen, especially Salesmen for Apparel, both new and old." [10] Aldersgate Street was "well-built and inhabited, except at the West End, of some Trade for Button-Mould-Makers".[11] Dyers, upholsterers, hat, boot and shoe makers, leather cutters, woollen and linen drapers, hosiers, stocking trimmers, feather manufacturers, wholesale haberdashers, ribbon weavers, calico-glazers, cambric waterers and a "lace and mode warehouse"[12] were all based in the vicinity. Cripplegate was also reputed to have more barbers' shops than anywhere else in London.

At the edge of Cripplegate Glasshouse Yard, off Aldersgate, marks the site of a neighbourhood so entirely obscure it is hard to explain why it existed. The Liberty of Glasshouse Yard was the tiniest of a series of miniature districts called Liberties, beyond the City walls. A glass factory operated here in the 16th and 17th centuries, hence the name, and the Liberty was originally an outlying section of St. Botolph-without-Aldgate parish, to the east. The expansion of London beyond the City walls created areas that eventually became self-governing parishes in their own right. Despite consisting of nothing but a tiny number of small alleys, the Liberty had a population of around 1,000 people when it became a parish of its own in 1866. It remained a unit of local government until it was abolished in 1915, when the parishes of Finsbury were finally reorganised.

The former Whitbread Brewery on Chiswell Street is one of the few buildings in Cripplegate to survive the Blitz. It was first set up in the Goat Brewhouse on Whitecross Street in 1742, before moving to a larger disused brewhouse on Chiswell Street. A new, more modern brewery was built on the site and survived with alterations and expansion until 1976, when brewing came to an end. The smell from the brewery was one of the defining features of Cripplegate for 200 years, particularly so on Mondays when the brewery vessels were cleaned out and the odour was both unmistakeable and unpleasant.

In the 1850s, 14,000 people lived in Cripplegate, but as the 19th century ended, it was becoming more industrial and less residential. The Whitbread Brewery complex expanded into adjacent streets, and the south end of Bunhill Row was "all warehouse and factories" with the Churchill Home on Chiswell Street offering accommodation "for the better class of factory girl."[13]

Cripplegate also had a reputation as something of a maze, well before the notoriously confusing Barbican Estate was built. A character in Charles Dickens' *Martin Chuzzlewit* can be found "bewildering himself in Barbican"[14] in 1844. Cripplegate was "that labyrinth of narrow streets with towering buildings, which lies between Fore Street and Cheapside where railway vans for ever block the road, and great bales of 'soft' goods monopolize the pavements.'[15] In the 1890s courts remained off Whitecross Street with steep wooden staircases, red-tiled houses, washing hanging over the street, and broken windows.

Great Fires

Cripplegate's main problem, that eventually proved its downfall, was its combustibility. Throughout its history, major fires destroyed significant buildings and eventually the entire area, twice. Fires were not uncommon in the wooden buildings of medieval London, and Cripplegate certainly had its fair share. St. Giles Cripplegate had to be partially rebuilt after a fire in 1545. St. Agnes and St. Anne on Noble Street was gutted in 1548. The Fortune Theatre burned down 1621. It was rebuilt, in brick this time, but burned down again in 1649.

Cripplegate's churches suffered greatly during the Great Fire of 1666, and again in the Blitz. St. Agnes and St. Anne was destroyed in the Great Fire, along with St. John Zachary, St. Mary Staining Oat Lane and St. Peter Westcheap, of which only churchyards survive. The tower is all that remains of St. Alban Wood Lane. St. Mary Aldermanbury was burned down in 1666 and again in 1940. Its ruins were removed in 1966 and re-erected in Fulton, Missouri as a peculiar memorial to Winston Churchill, and its garden is all that is left. St. Stephen Coleman Street was also destroyed in the Blitz, but the apparently bombed ruins of St. Alphage London Wall actually date

St. Anne and St. Agnes Church, Gresham Street

from its partial demolition in 1923.

The Great Fire of 1660 burned all of Cripplegate within the City but stopped at the walls, leaving Cripplegate Without untouched. However, Cripplegate Without was not so lucky when the next fire came along. On the afternoon of 20th November 1897 fire broke out in an ostrich feather warehouse on Well Street, a site now deep under the Barbican. The surrounding streets were packed with rag trade warehouses, housing highly inflammable goods: cotton, silk and wool, drapery and millinery, boots, umbrellas, gloves, bags, "fancy stationery", "tobacco pouches"[16] and, of course, feathers. Cripplegate was coloured red, for very high risk, on contemporary insurance maps, and the warehouse district was known as 'Fire Island'.

Three hundred firemen fought the flames, but soon 17 entire streets were burning and by the time the fire was out, more than a hundred warehouses had been destroyed. A journalist wrote "There were blazing shops and warehouses on either side, brickwork and debris of every kind were crashing down everywhere, and the heat was terrific. I got saturated to the skin over and over again, but I only had to go and stand in front of a blazing shop to dry my clothes."[17] Contemporary reports claimed 4,000 people, mostly women, were put out of work as a result and the price of ostrich feathers rose by 30 per cent. An area equivalent to the entire western half of the Barbican Estate was destroyed.

Both the Surgeon Barbers' Hall and St. Giles Church were saved by firemen but they were not, unfortunately, able to repeat the feat 50 years later. A photograph of the aftermath shows St. Giles standing alone, again, among the devastation, a premonition of further destruction to come. The tinderbox nature of Cripplegate was underlined in April 1902, when a fire described as the biggest in London since the 1897 blaze broke out in MacQueen's Hat Factory and spread to Aldersgate, threatening the underground station (then called Aldersgate, now Barbican). Several warehouses on the now lost Australian and New Zealand Avenues were gutted, and houses and shops burned down.

Bomb site

Given the area's previous record, it was particularly vulnerable when the Blitz began. However, even before the war the omens were not good. The Auxiliary Fire Service, preparing for raids, carried out its first major exercise in 1938 in Cripplegate based at Redcross Street Fire Station. It did not go well. The appropriately named Aylmer Firebrace, Chief Officer of the London Fire Brigade, reported that "The exercise had already started, though you could hardly tell by the indifferent poses of the telephonists. There were fires in Jewin Crescent, fires in London Wall, fires in Silver Street... by early morning the overflowing offices, warehouses and sweatshops of 'Fire Island' had proved too much for the well-meaning amateurs of the Auxiliary Fire Service. The independent referees announced that the fires had won. Theoretically the Barbican was burning all around them."[18]

When the bombs came for real, the scenario was pretty much the same. Relatively few people were killed, but the damage was huge. The whole of Cripplegate was almost completely destroyed, and a band of devastation stretched from Cripplegate to the Thames, with St. Paul's Cathedral an island in the middle. A blitzed strip, more than a mile long and half a mile wide, was once filled with the densest network of streets in the capital.

Richard Trench describes the morning after the bombs fell: "It was 9.00 am, Monday morning. The wind had died down and a million fragments of ash and embers snowed down on them. The tarmac in the road was still burning in places. A few walls, strengthened by their chimneys, stood like headstones. The remaining buildings were ghosts, their positions marked by piles of rubble. Only the shell of St Giles', Whitbread's Brewery and irony upon ironies – Redcross Street Fire Station – stood upright. South of St Giles' along London Wall stretches of the Roman wall revealed themselves for the first time in 200 years."[19] The Whitbread Brewery survived thanks to the efforts of its own in-house fire brigade, who extinguished the hundreds of incendiaries that hit the building. Post-war photographs show the brewery standing alone, the Cripplegate streets in the foreground entirely levelled.

There was irony in the destruction visited on a manufacturing city: "The sub-officer in charge came in carrying an unexploded incendiary. On it was its date and the firm's stamp. It had been made in 1938 by an engineering company in Islington, who had exported fire bombs to Germany right up to the declaration of war."[20]

The Blitz ended but Cripplegate remained in ruins, partly used by the Home Guard to practise fighting in a bombed-out city. The landscape returned, to some extent, to the heathland it must have been before

St. Giles Cripplegate Church

London grew across it. It was the ultimate adventure playground for London children, a bombsite bigger than any other. Wild plants took over: "Grass grows here, covering, healing, and russet sorrel in tall spikes, and golden rod, swaying beside broken walls, full of butterflies, and purple loose-strife, and one plant, willow herb, that some people call fireweed."[21] Rosebay willow herb, also known as fireweed, is often the first plant to grow after fire. It colonised the charred city in 1666, after the Great Fire of London, and it returned after 1940, sometimes described as the Second Great Fire of London.

Marginal characters, appropriately for Cripplegate, began to live and roam around the ruined cellars and basements. Rose Macaulay's *The World My Wilderness* describes crossing the ruins: "They skirted a massive bastion of wall, broken, tree-grown, assaulted by casualty of war, and later by that of demolition men; crossing Barber's Hall, that gaping chasm where fireweed ran over Inigo Jones's court room."[22]

Rebuilding

Bombing accelerated change that had been coming more gradually, with the declining small workshops that were disappearing from the City anyway swept away in a night, never to return. By 1951 only 48 people were registered as living within the Cripplegate ward, so widespread was the damage.

Many Cripplegate streets, destroyed in the Blitz, were wiped from the map. Several streets lost their companions: Whitecross Street, Silk Street and Golden Lane survived, but Redcross Street, Paper Street and Silver Street did not. Both Australian and New Zealand Avenues disappeared, as did Jewin Crescent and Jewin Street, at the heart of the neighbourhood. The street called Barbican became part of Beech Street after rebuilding. A short street called Short Street vanished from the map as did, among many others, Cripplegate Street, Great Arthur Street, Lilypot Lane, Oat Lane, Playhouse Yard and Red Lion Market.

The fact that these streets no longer exist was a planning decision rather than a direct consequence of the bombing. Parts of the bombed street pattern were recreated, but those that lay on the site of the Barbican were subsumed into a new vision of London. The Barbican was built as a prototype for the future City which would be layered, with pedestrians separated on walkways from the traffic in the streets below. This thinking is exemplified in the walk from Barbican tube station to the Barbican Arts Centre, which can be conducted either at first floor level via spacious but labyrinthine walkways, or through the traffic tunnel that is Beech Street.

The Barbican is in fact the most substantial remnant of the City of London's Pedway scheme which, from the 1960s, required new buildings to incorporate first floor space that could be used as part of a walkway network. Large sections were built in places such as

London Wall and Lower Thames Street, but by the 1980s fashions had changed and the huge scheme was dropped, leaving strange dead-ends and unused bridges which can be found across the City to this day. The Barbican is the only place where it is possible to see what the finished result might have looked like. As London's least navigable place it is a poor advertisement for walkways, but it is like no other part of the City and in places the walker feels suspended in mid-air.

The Barbican Estate grew up very gradually in 35 acres of blitzed Cripplegate, which lay derelict for 13 years before a plan was eventually approved for the Golden Lane Estate. It was designed by architects Chamberlin, Powell and Bon, who built their vision of the future on the ruins of Great Arthur Street, Hatfield Street and the ancient courts in between. Their designs were a vision of a future entirely different to the Cripplegate they replaced, abandoning streets in favour of multiple levels, walkways and wide open spaces. Great Arthur House was the tallest block of flats in Europe at the time. Towers and walkways soon appeared in various forms across the Western world, but they work better here than almost anywhere else and the estate has proved a very popular place to live, not least for architects. Ian Nairn said of the estate "This is no ivory tower",[23] and despite 30 years of tenants' 'right to buy' their council flats, half of Golden Lane remains public housing.

When it came to the Barbican Chamberlin, Powell and Bon, whose success at Golden Lane gained them the job that would consume most of their careers, created something rather closer to an ivory tower. At one point the entire complex was to have been clad in white marble. Instead, they opted for the complete opposite, poured concrete. Astonishingly, every inch of surface was pick-axed by hand for a rough finish. The Barbican included the tallest residential tower blocks in Europe, 43 stories high and the sheer size of the estate, an entire neighbourhood in itself, reflected the resources available to its unusually wealthy owner, the Corporation of London. It was also intended to tower socially over its Golden Lane neighbour, with a minimum income required to qualify for a flat.

More uncompromising post-war development sprung up around the edges of the Barbican, particularly on London Wall where six almost identical 18-storey blocks were lined up during the 1960s, subsequently much-altered and rebuilt. Construction began at the Barbican in 1964 and the three towers, Cromwell, Lauderdale and Shakespeare, were finished in the mid-1970s. However, by the time the Barbican Arts Centre opened in 1982, completing the new Cripplegate, the old version had been largely forgotten. The Barbican is infamously difficult to navigate, and the painted yellow line or golden thread required to reach the arts centre in its depths lends a mythological air to its maze. However, it should be no surprise that a complex named the Barbican resembles a defensive fortification and, once inside, a self-enclosed world awaits, the white noise of the fountains closing out the city beyond the walls. St. Giles Cripplegate sits on a concrete peninsula surrounded by lakes, a projection from a past London and the only substantial evidence of the place that has disappeared.

The Barbican still feels like the future, albeit an alternative path that history chose not to take. It looks likely to continue on its own parallel course, an increasingly separate world stirring faint nostalgia for the utopian dreams of the past. There is, though, the suspicion that the whole edifice is a fantasy, and that one day it will collapse, undermined by the restless, shifting Cripplegate streets buried beneath its vast superstructure.

REFERENCES

1   Black, Jeremy, *London*, London: Carnegie Publishing (2009)
2   Sinclair, Iain, *Lights Out for the Territory*, Granta 1997

3   Denton, W, *Records of St Giles' Cripplegate*, 1883

4   http://johnsonsdictionaryonline.com/

5   Rogers, Pat, *Hacks and Dunces: Pope, Swift and Grub Street*, University Paperbacks 1972

6   Strype, John, *A Survey of the Cities of London and Westminster*, 1720

7   Turner, E.S. *Unholy Pursuits: The Wayward Parsons of Grub Street*, The Book Guild Ltd. 1998

8   Denton, W, *Records of St Giles' Cripplegate*, 1883

9   Hughson (1802) quoted in Thornbury, Walter, *Old and New London: Volume 2*, Cassell (1879)

10   Strype, John, *A Survey of the Cities of London and Westminster*, 1720

11   Maitland, William, *The history of London from its foundation to the present time ... including the several parishes in Westminster, Middlesex, Southwark, &c., within the bills of mortality*, J. Wilkie (1775)

12   Baddeley, Sir John, *Cripplegate: one of the twenty-six wards of the City of London*, Hodder & Stoughton (1922)

13   Booth, Charles, *Survey Into Life and Labour in London 1886-1903*, LSE Charles Booth Online Archive

14   Dickens, Charles, *Martin Chuzzlewit*, Penguin (2000, originally published 1844)

15   Blyth, Harry (1894) 'The Accusing Shadow' in Cox, M. ed. *The Oxford Book of Victorian Detective Stories*, Oxford University Press (2003)

16   *The Brisbane Courier*, 20th November 1897

17   http://airforceamazons.blogspot.co.uk/2010/09/fireweed.html accessed 23 January 2014

18   Trench, Richard, *London Before the Blitz*, Weidenfeld & Nicolson (1989)

19   *ibid*

20   *ibid*

21   Paton Walsh, Jill, *Fireweed*, Puffin (1972)

22   Macaulay, Rose, *The World My Wilderness*, Penguin (1958)

23   Nairn, Ian, *Nairn's London*, Penguin 1966

HORSELYDOWN, ST. OLAVE AND PICKLE HERRING

A district of wharves and warehouses, known as 'London's Larder', once filled the area between London Bridge and Tower Bridge.

Introduction

Although it is just a step away from London's most famous bridge, few Londoners could guess at the location of Horselydown. Still fewer know a street called Pickle Herring. The neighbourhoods of London Bridge have been realigned since the days when Southwark's main thoroughfare was the River Thames. A district of wharves and warehouses, known as 'London's Larder', once filled the area between London Bridge and Tower Bridge. The western part, at the foot of London Bridge, was known as St. Olave, while the eastern end at Tower Bridge was called Horselydown. Along the river ran Pickle Herring, the archetypal London dock street tightly packed with warehouses, criss-crossed by iron bridges and hung with hoists.

As the Port of London and its ships faded away, the neighbourhood became a very different proposition, swapping heavy industry for civic buildings and accountancy firms. By the end of the 20th century the old waterfront had been almost entirely erased. Dark, narrow, noisy Pickle Herring was swept from the map, replaced by the hard landscaping and office wedges of the 'More London' development and the bulbous new City Hall. The metamorphosis was finalised with the construction of The Shard, Europe's tallest building and the centrepiece of the relabelled 'London Bridge Quarter'. Horselydown and St. Olave no longer form part of the picture.

The Horse Down

Southwark was London's first suburb, just over the water from the City and dating back to the Romans. From its earliest days Tooley Street ran parallel to the Thames, known in the Tudor era as 'Short Southwark' to distinguish it from Borough High Street, or 'Long Southwark'. The pocket-sized settlement may have possessed only two significant streets, but its location at the southern end of London Bridge made it an important strategic and commercial entrance to the City of London.

Southwark once ended where Tower Bridge Road is now, Tooley Street running into fields known as Horselydown. Variations on its spelling include Horsa Downe, Horsy Downe and Horse Down, and it was clearly fields used for grazing. It may in fact have been an eyot, an island raised above damp surroundings and bounded by vanished tidal channels. The pre-medieval Thames was a slower, wider river and at high tide it lapped the Old Kent Road, while the undrained south bank fragmented into a series of islands and streams. St. Saviour's Creek, which survives downstream from Tower Bridge, may have formed the eastern channel around the Horselydown eyot. It is also the last unburied section of the Neckinger River (see the author's *London's Lost Rivers*).[1]

Most of Horselydown and the parish of St. Olave were in the Liberty of St. John, land owned by the Hospital of St. John of Jerusalem in Clerkenwell. Part of the Horselydown pastures, however, belonged to the monks of Bermondsey Abbey which lay immediately to the south, at the end of Bermondsey Street. The Abbot's lands were seized by Henry VIII and the Abbey demolished in 1541. A rood (a large crucifix) was rescued from the Abbey church and re-erected on the open fields of Horselydown. It was taken down in 1559, but survives in street name form as Crucifix Lane.

When the monasteries were dissolved the Abbey's estates passed to the Crown, and were eventually granted to the Corporation of London by Edward VI in 1550. As a result the south side of London Bridge became part of the City of London, despite being on the wrong side of the river. It was given its own City ward, Bridge Without, mirroring the Bridge Within ward at the northern end of London Bridge. However, unlike every other City ward it never elected Councilmen, so remained in a state of administrative limbo.

The official boundaries of the City were finally redrawn to exclude Bridge Without in 1899, but the City carried on appointing an alderman to oversee the non-existent ward until 1978, when the entirely notional territory was merged back into the City. However, the City of London still retains the whole of London Bridge within its boundaries, a relic of the time when buildings ran across its full length.

Norse London

St. Olave's Church, once at the junction of Tooley Street and Duke Street Hill, was dedicated to King Olaf II of Norway, canonised in the 12th century as St. Olaf. His support helped to oust the Danish King Cnut in 1014, restoring Ethelred the Unready to the English throne. With the Danes holding London Bridge against English and Norse forces encamped in Sudvirke (Southwark), Olaf's ships sailed under the bridge, tied cables around the supports, and tore it and the

Danes down. Olaf became a martyr after his death in battle in 1030, and a number of London churches were dedicated to him. The name Tooley Street is also thought to derive from a corrupted version of the saint's name.

The church's dedication is the sole evidence of a Viking presence in south London, but it may mean that there was a Norse enclave for a time in this part of Southwark. The first reference to St. Olave's Church is in fact in *Heimskringla* or *The Lives of the Norse Kings*, Icelandic sagas written in the early 1200s by Snorri Sturlason. He tells the tale of a crippled man visited in a dream by a man who advised him "Go thou to St Olav's Church which is in London and there thou wilt be healed".[2] He travelled from France to London where a stranger guided him as he crawled across London Bridge. On entering St. Olave's "he rose up immediately, sound and strong" miraculously healed, but his companion had mysteriously vanished.

In the middle ages, Tooley Street marked the edge of built-up London south of the Thames, and was the location of choice for noblemen looking for space to build and expand their mansions. Edward II built himself a moated manor house in 1325, known as The Rosary, west of what is now Potters Fields. Nearby Battle Bridge Lane commemorates the town mansion of the Abbot of Battle in Sussex. This was one of several large houses in the vicinity belonging to clerics, which also included the manor houses of the Abbot of St. Augustine's in Canterbury and the Prior of Lewes, and was on a site now covered by Hay's Wharf. After Battell House was confiscated from the Abbot at the dissolution of the monasteries its grounds became gardens, where locals in the late 16th century recalled bowling and playing quoits.

Horselydown Fair

John Stow, writing in the 1590s, describes "Saint Olaves street having continuall building on both the sides, with lanes and alleyes up to

The London Dungeon, Tooley Street

Battle bridge, to Horsedowne, and towardes Rother hith." However, London still ended at the Horselydown meadows. The open space at Horselydown was used by the inhabitants of St Olave's parish for grazing. A 'martial yard' and an 'artillery hall' were built on the south east side of the fields in 1636 and used by the local defensive militia, the Southwark Trained Bands. The drill hall was used until 1725 when it became St. Olave's Workhouse, and the Arnold Estate on Druid Street now occupies the site.

A 1570 painting, 'A Fête at Bermondsey' by Joris Hoefnagel (now kept at Hatfield House) shows a fair at Horselydown. The Tower of London can be seen on the horizon, across the Thames, and the fair is attended by well-dressed promenaders. Trees and fields surround the fair, with just a cluster of buildings at the centre, occupying the site where St. John Horselydown Church was later constructed.

Fair Street was built across the Horselydown pastures in the mid-1600s, and its name is probably a reference to the same 'fête' as the painting. Having begun on Horselydown, by the 1660s it had moved to a different site in Borough and became known as Southwark or St. Margaret's Fair. Until it was suppressed in 1763 it was a famous London attraction, with Bartholomew and St. James' one of London's three great fairs. Hogarth painted it as a scene of chaotic theatre, with acrobats, monkeys and tumbling spectators. Samuel Pepys described the Fair as "very dirty", while John Evelyn enthusiastically described seeing "monkies and asses dance and do other feates of activity on ye tight rope". He also enjoyed "a man who tooke up a piece of iron cannon of about 400 lb. weight, with the haire of his head onely", and "a monstrous birth of Twinns, both femals & most perfectly shaped, save that they were joyn'd breast to breast, & incorporated at the navil."[3]

Horselydown began to change when the Governors of St. Olave's School developed the fields they owned, building brick houses at St. Saviour's Dock in the 1660s which they let out to seamen. When its population began to grow, the eastern half of St. Olave was separated out in 1733 to form a new parish called Horselydown. A new church was built on an area of the pastures that had been used by the trained bands.

St. John Horselydown was one of the last of the new churches built under Queen Anne, intended to bring a Church of England presence to the new London suburbs and fight the rise of nonconformity. The result was a cousin to Hawksmoor's St. Luke's Old Street. Both churches were classical buildings with strange Ionic columns as spires: "An obelisk to loom about the bridges, streets, and lives that teem therein. Above their minds, their dreams, six generations to its shadow born."[4] On top, a gilded weather vane of a peculiar shape flew with the breeze. Although it was in fact a comet, from ground level it seemed to resemble an insect and so St. John's was known as 'the lousy church'.

Brewers and tailors

By the 16th century Southwark was famous for its beer. Flemish Protestant refugees arrived in London escaping persecution of Protestants during the 1560s, and so many settled in Southwark that the burial grounds at St. Olave's Church became known as the Flemish Churchyard. Flemish immigrants set up in the brewing trade, taking advantage of access to Thames water with breweries on the riverfront, and may have been responsible for introducing hops to flavour beer. The river from London Bridge to Horselydown became a succession of breweries.

One of the Flemish arrivals, Henry Leake, owned the Dolphin Brewhouse as well as the Beare pub at the foot of the bridge. In 1560 he left money in his will to found St. Olave's Free Grammar School, which educated Horselydown for the next 400 years. One of its early headmasters was Robert Browne, in charge during the 1580s, a notorious religious separatist imprisoned 32 times for his non-conformist beliefs. He was known as the 'Father of the Pilgrims' because many of those who left England on The Mayflower had been 'Brownists'.

The beer produced by Vassal Webling, another Flemish brewer, was considered so potent that the Governors of St. Thomas's Hospital became concerned. They recorded that "the house beer is too strong and begets a taste", and that even the hospital matron had succumbed to it.[5]

The only surviving Horselydown brewery is the former Anchor Brewhouse on Shad Thames, later known as the Courage Brewery, a distinctively chaotic, turreted building which is scarcely noticeable from Shad Thames but entirely unmissable from the river. It was converted into flats in the late 1980s, during the first phase of docklands regeneration, but the Anchor Tap pub, which was the brewery pub, still operates on Horselydown Lane.

The Anchor Brewhouse is easily confused with the Anchor

The Anchor Brewhouse, Shad Thames

Brewery, a larger, more famous facility owned by Barclay Perkins & Co., on Park Street, on the other side of Borough Market, which was demolished in 1981. Barclay Perkins merged with Courage in 1955 and it too became the Courage Brewery, making it even harder to tell the two apart.

On Potter's Fields

The Flemish inhabitants of Horselydown were also involved in the pottery industry for which the area was famous during the 16th and 17th centuries. The original seems to have been the Pickleherring Pottery, on a site roughly where the Scoop is today, next to City Hall. A Dutchman called Christian Wilhelm opened it in 1618, making an English version of the Delftware famously produced in Holland. It also made Galleyware – jugs and tableware – which was clearly high quality as Charles I appointed Wilhelm 'Royal Gallypot Maker' in 1628. The industry expanded, with 124 potters recorded in St. Olave's Parish during the course of the 1600s. The Pickleherring Pottery later moved to Horselydown, where it was called the White Pot House, and closed in the 1770s by which time the potteries had all disappeared. A 1965 archaeological dig on Potter's Fields unearthed two tons of discarded pottery shards.

The open space that exists today at Potter's Fields would seem, at first glance, to be directly related to the potters who worked there. However, a 'potter's field' also has an entirely separate meaning as a generic term for a place where unknown people, and suicides, are buried. It originates in the Bible as the piece of ground bought by the Chief Priest with Judas' 30 pieces of silver to "bury strangers in", and known as "the field of blood".[6] Potter's Fields also contained a burial ground, shared between the two churches of St. Olave and St. John Horselydown, so it may be that the name has both figurative and literal meaning. The burial ground later became the playground of St. Olave's School.

Although now a park again, Potter's Fields were built over as Horselydown developed. Wharves replaced potteries, and by the start of the 20th century it was home to wool warehouses and storehouses. There was also a doss-house, where George Orwell stayed in 1930 while researching *Down and Out in London and Paris*. Orwell met a man called Ginger in the Kentish hop-fields and walked to London with him, where they spent three weeks living in the Tooley Street 'kip'. This informed his description of the grim London doss houses, with their "sweetish reek of paregoric and foul linen", where "loathsome coughing"[7] kept him up all night, and "bread and marge" was the difference between survival and starvation. Orwell wrote some of the book in St. Olave's Branch Library, on Potter's Fields, which was demolished in the 1980s.

Bridge and tunnel

The coherence and identity of St. Olave and Horselydown were threatened as soon as London's first railway terminus opened at London Bridge in 1836. The first railway line ran just four miles to Greenwich, but was very popular for daytrips to the park and pubs of Greenwich where whitebait dinners were a famous treat.

The marshy ground on the south side of the river meant that railway lines had to be built on a long viaduct, which bisects the neighbourhood from east to west. The arches that march across Horselydown quickly came to define the space around them, creating a series of long, dark tunnels running south from Tooley Street under the railway – forbidding, neglected vaults. Their reputation was sealed by two separate Second World War disasters: direct hits on both the Druid Street and Stainer Street arches which were being used as air raid shelters, in which many people were killed.

The only route across the river until the 19th century was London Bridge, notoriously congested, so the watermen who ferried passengers were very popular. River steps at Battle Bridge and Horselydown were used to take people across the Thames, or row sailors to their ships at anchor. Horselydown Steps, used by watermen until the First World War, survive beneath the Anchor Brewery and are perhaps the most complete reminder of the old riverfront, an unnoticed archway leading to the Thames shore under Tower Bridge. Horselydown's identity was maintained by the watermen who worked the steps. Teams from the Thames neighbourhoods competed in an annual regatta, from Bankside, Deptford, Greenwich, Horselydown, Rotherhithe, and Wapping. An account from 1902 gives a clear picture of how active, and dangerous, the Thames still was: "At Horselydown Stairs, the men are busy. They are rowing wharfingers across the stream, and seamen to their ships. A waterman's life is a busy one for a few months of the year. He commences his work early in the morning and ceases late at night. He runs many risks. At times he is in danger of being run down by a passenger steamer, or he is run into by a barge and capsized; yet comparatively few among them can swim. Scarcely a week passes without an inquest on the body of a waterman or lighterman who was drowned while engaged in his work."[8]

Tower Bridge, built between 1886 and 1894, included a new approach road, Tower Bridge Road, which sliced straight through the middle of Horselydown. This required the demolition of Davis Wharf, Hartley Wharf, and several streets. The change this brought to Horselydown was lamented in 1927, through rose-tinted spectacles that looked back to Hoefnagel's painting of Bermondsey Fair: "Instead of the delightful group of a village inn and clustering cottages, we now only find such commercial highways such as Tooley Street and Tower Bridge Road cutting the little network of streets where the dense, industrial population now lives."[9]

Another river crossing from Horselydown is locked away under the river. The Tower Subway was built in 1871, as no-one had been able to design a bridge that would allow shipping to pass underneath. Passengers originally travelled on a rope-drawn train but it was too expensive, and the company running the tunnel went bankrupt. The train was withdrawn and only foot traffic allowed, at a cheaper rate. One million people paid the toll to cross until the free Tower Bridge made it redundant. The tunnel closed in 1898, but still exists and is now used for water mains. Its south bank entrance is now hidden behind the Unicorn Theatre on Tooley Street.

The industrial nature of the neighbourhood is spectacularly illustrated by the Tooley Street fire. The streets on the river side of Tooley Street were narrow and crowded, and many of the houses were still made of wood. On 22nd June 1861 the entire neighbourhood went up in flames when a warehouse at Cotton's Wharf caught fire. Burning tallow, tar, resin and oil stored in the warehouses floated, blazing, down the Thames and set small craft alight. The goods in storage fed the fire which burned for two weeks and continued to smoulder for three months, the largest conflagration in London since the Great Fire, 200 years before. Thames bridges were so crowded with onlookers watching the fire and the explosions that several people fell into the river and were drowned. It is said that for months afterwards people waded into the Thames to skim off the floating oil.

There was no public fire service in London at the time, only the London Fire Engine Establishment funded by insurance companies. On the corner of Braidwood Street is a memorial to its director, James Braidwood, who died when a wall collapsed on him while he was fighting the fire. Braidwood was a Scotsman who had founded the first city fire service in Edinburgh before coming to London. His death, and the scale of the Tooley Street disaster, led eventually to the founding of the London Fire Brigade.

London's larder

At its peak, the streets of Horselydown were home to a densely packed working population. Main streets, such as Tooley Street, housed respectable offices, but housing was often in poor condition and crowded, squeezed between railway viaducts and the many factories and workshops of the area. Charles Booth reported in 1898 that Barnham Street was said to have "the dirtiest, noisiest, worst-paying tenants in London."[10] With a dog food factory as a neighbour, and with the street semi-demolished to widen the railway lines, Barnham Street cannot have been the choicest place to live. The encroachments on Horselydown and St. Olave from Tower Bridge Road, the constantly expanding railway and the developing wharves and factories meant that houses had low priority, and the neighbourhood became increasingly dilapidated and obscure as the 19th century came to an end.

The mainstay of the local economy was the Thames, and the intense industry of Horselydown focused on the wharves where for centuries a huge array of perishable and dry goods had been unloaded.

The Tooley Street warehouses handled much of the food brought to London by sea. In 1920, *The Graphic* wrote that "all the available space between London Bridge and Tower Bridge is devoted in the main to the storage and distribution of merchandise. Dutch cheese, Swiss milk and Danish butter are accompanied by German pianos, which arrive there regularly in steamers from the Continent."[11] Photographs from the 1930s show Horselydown from the river, cranes, jetties and steamers at anchor and a wall of warehouses and wharves. Between London Bridge and Tower Bridge there was a continuous wall of 18 separate wharves. Battlebridge Stairs and Pickle Herring Stairs provided the only pedestrian access to the river along the entire stretch.

The most famous wharf on the south side of the river was Hay's, which is still intact, rebuilt after the 1861 fire for which it was responsible. It became known for importing tea, and at one point 80 per cent of London's dry goods imports were said to pass through Hay's Wharf. It was also where Ernest Shackleton's ship The Quest lay in 1921, before sailing for the South Atlantic on his final, fatal voyage.

Horselydown was a place of business not pleasure, and was obscure even at the height of its importance. A late 19th century description explains that "Of all the quarters and parts of London, that of Horselydown is the least known and least visited except by those whose business takes them there every day. There is, in fact, nothing to be seen; the wharves block out the river, the warehouses darken the streets, the places where people live are not interesting; there is not an ancient memory or association or any ancient fragment of a building to make one desire to visit Horselydown." The oppressive atmosphere of the wharves clearly made an impression on visitors.

Pickled herrings

At the heart of the Horselydown riverfront was Pickle Herring, one of

Traces of St. Olave's Church, Tooley Street

London's great lost streets. It is easy to imagine what Pickle Herring was like because it was a continuation westwards of Shad Thames, running parallel to the Thames all the way from Tower Bridge to Hay's Dock. Blanchard Jerrold, assessing Pickle Herring in 1872, sees nothing out of the ordinary about the street: "At the cost of sundry blows and much buffeting from the hastening crowds we make notes of Pickle-Herring Street: now pushed to the road, and now driven against the wall. The hard-visaged men, breathlessly competing for 'dear life,' glance, mostly with an eye of wondering pity, at the sketcher, and at his companion with the note-book. What, in the name of common-sense, can we want with old Pickle-Herring Street, that has been just the same as it is time out of mind?"[12] Gustav Doré's accompanying illustration shows a Dante-esque scene with storey upon storey of arches and hoists, where tiny figures of men balance on high platforms guiding never-ending loads.

The origins of the name are mysterious. On the one hand, Pickle Herring was apparently a Dutch term for a buffoon in use during the 16th century. Later, the Horselydown parish registers record the death in 1854 of Peter Van Durrante, alias "Pickell Herringe, brewer". But perhaps its use as an affectionate insult came from the amount of pickled herring landed here. It was a delicacy, traded with France in the Middle Ages for Bordeaux wines, which were otherwise only available in exchange for gold. Sir John Falstolf, who was born in Great Yarmouth, shipped Yarmouth herrings to London. Falstolf's commercial herring interests partly explain the famous Battle of the Herrings in 1429. This involved Falstolf, who was bringing supplies including herrings to the English army besieging Orleans, defeated an attack by a combined French and Scots force. His line in fish is surely no coincidence, and eventually he came to own Pickle Herring as part of his Southwark estates. In Shakespeare's *Twelfth Night* Sir Toby Belch, engaged in a Falstaffian drinking session, complains "A plague o' these pickle-herring".

Sir John Falstolf has since been eclipsed by his fictional namesake. Shakespeare is thought to have based his character on a different knight, Sir John Oldcastle, but was forced to make a last-minute name change when Oldcastle's family took exception to their ancestor being portrayed as the Lord of Misrule. The real Falstolf was a commander in the Hundred Years War, fighting the French and Joan of Arc. He owned a house called Falstolf Place on Tooley Street, and large amounts of property in St. Olave's parish including water mills, tenements, a garden called 'Le Walles' and three beer houses: 'Le Bores Head' (perhaps the tavern featured in Shakespeare), 'Le Harte Horne' and the 'High Bere House', which was still standing in 1560. Appropriately, it is thought to have been sited near the present-day Anchor Brewery at Horselydown.

Shad Thames is at the centre of what remains of Horselydown today and is itself a remarkable street, catnip to the tourist with its cobbles and picturesque iron bridges. Despite being hugely scrubbed up from its working days when it was "narrow, badly paved and dirty... full of flour, corn and rice merchants and mills",[13] it is still intensely redolent of a different time. Just like Pickle Herring it also has a mysterious, fishy name, which may relate to shad, a river version of the herring. The idea of a Shad Thames three times as long is overwhelming, and suggests that London lost something important when it let Pickle Herring go.

Two lost churches

In 1920, despite signs that the traditional river traffic in the Pool of London was in decline, Hay's Wharf engaged in a massive expansion programme. Its owners bought up the neighbouring wharves – Chamberlain's, Cotton's, Fenning's, Nestlé, and Sun – for modernisation. The reconstructed wharves were designed to allow larger ships to be unloaded faster, without needing to use lighters. As part of this expansion, and to allow Tooley Street to be widened, St. Olave's Church was demolished. *The Graphic* helpfully commented that "Any resentment at the demolition of St. Olave's Church, which is sanctioned by a recent Act of Parliament, may be dispelled by the knowledge that the building is useless."[14] However, it was the wharves which would be redundant within 40 years. Despite the unfortunate demise of the church, its replacement St. Olaf's House, offices for Hay's Wharf, is one of the most striking pieces of Art Deco design in London, by the architect H.S. Goodhart-Rendel.

St. Olave's was not the only church to be demolished in the area. The lousy spire of St. John, next to the railway lines, was a familiar landmark to passengers arriving at London Bridge Station from Kent and Surrey. Its disappearance from the skyline is one of the reasons Horselydown has been forgotten. The church was gutted during the Second World War and left roofless, but its spire remained standing exactly as happened at St. Luke's Old Street. This symmetry did not escape Iain Sinclair, who wrote about the two churches and the destroyed St. Mary Matfellon in Whitechapel as "The three enclosures of ruin. Unacknowledged, but not concealed. St Luke, roofless, wild space in a border of stone; St. John, a rim of the original on to which a place of business has been grafted; and Mary Matfellon, nothing, a field with a diagram in the grass... The less they are, the stranger they become."[15]

The ruins of St. Luke's were restored after decades left open to the elements, but St. John was demolished in the 1970s. The money allocated to rebuild it was spent on a church for the Abbey Estate in Abbey Wood, in South East London, as inner city residents moved out to new estates. In 1975 Naismith House, the offices of the London City Mission, opened on its footprint. The lost church at the heart of Horselydown still feels present, its graveyard and stone foundations intact. Sinclair's description of the Hawksmoor churches as "slack dynamos abandoned as the culture they supported goes into retreat"[16] fits the missing neighbourhood, its people and purpose rubbed away by time. The golden louse was taken down in 1948, but can be seen in a display case inside the London City Mission.

Endgame

From the 1960s London docklands entered a rapid and terminal decline, leaving areas of the city deserted and semi-derelict. In the decades before redevelopment, St. Olave and Horselydown, like many of London's riverside neighbourhoods, entered a state of suspended animation. Noel Spencer's painting, *Pickle Herring Street, London* (1961) shows a narrow, deserted street save for a single under-occupied man, leaning on a bollard beneath a 'Mind the Cranes' sign. The Southwark Borough Librarian wrote in 1973 that "At present the neighbourhood consists almost entirely of wharves and warehouses, although many of these are now disused and being demolished."[17] A visitor in 1972 was surprised to find no traffic at all on Tooley Street, and reported that "The few rather empty shops are evidence that people do not live here if they can possibly get away. In fact it is only in Horselydown Lane itself where the restrained affluence of Courage's brewery shows any evidence of prosperity."[18]

St. Olave's Grammar School had closed in 1968, due to a shortage of pupils, as families moved away from poor and bombed inner city areas, in search of modern houses and jobs. The school followed former inhabitants of Horselydown out to Orpington, on the London fringe. The school building itself remains, redeveloped as a hotel after standing abandoned for years on the empty Potter's Fields.

As the regeneration of the Docklands began in the early 1980s, the warehouses north of Tooley Street were bought by St. Martin's Property, the real estate arm of the Emirate of Kuwait, which still owns this section of riverbank. They planned to develop it as 'London Bridge City', and began with the reopening of Hay's Wharf as Hay's Galleria, under a Victorian-style glass roof. The new Southwark Crown Court opened next door in 1983, taking over cases that had previously been heard at the Middlesex Guildhall Crown Court in Parliament Square. Potter's Fields were cleared, including the demolition of the Bethel Estate council houses.

However, plans for the largest site, where Pickle Herring had once been, ran into the sand. St. Martin's Property submitted a series of increasingly bizarre proposals in the late 1980s, including a huge pastiche development complete with a replica of the San Marco Tower in Venice, and something that appeared to be a copy of the Palace of Westminster.

Unsurprisingly, these last-days-of-post-modernism schemes were turned down, and the site remained empty until the 2000s when the current Norman Foster blocks were built. City Hall, built to house the new Mayor and Greater London Authority, opened in 2002 and for several years sat alone, in the middle of a large, derelict site.

Denmark House, Tooley Street

The offices occupying the site of the Pickle Herring wharves have replaced trade in food and dry goods with polished, knowledge economy floorspace. In the process the old places have slipped from consciousness, and Horselydown, St. Olave and Pickle Herring have become lost zones, squeezed out of their own neighbourhoods.

REFERENCES

1   Bolton, Tom, *London's Lost Rivers: a Walker's Guide*, Strange Attractor 2011

2   Sturlason, Snorri, *Heimskringla or the Lives of the Norse Kings,* Kessinger Publishing 2004

3   Evelyn, John, *The Diary of John Evelyn*, Oxford Clarendon Press 2000

4   Moore, Alan and Campbell, Eddie, *From Hell*, Knockabout 2006

5   Rendle, William & Norman, Philip, *The Inns of Old Southwark and their Associations*, Longmans & Co. 1888

6   Matthew 27: 7-10

7   Orwell, George, *Down and Out In Paris and London*, Penguin 1999

8   Moss, Arthur B. 'Waterside London' in G.R. Sims (ed.) *Living London: Its Work and Its Play, Its Humour and Its Pathos, Its Sights and Its Scenes,* Vol. 2 Cassell and Company 1902

9   *Country Life*, 12th February 1927

10   Booth, Charles, *Survey Into Life and Labour in London 1886-1903*, LSE Charles Booth Online Archive

11   *The Graphic*, 4th September 1920

12   Doré, Gustave and Jerrold, Blanchard, *London: A Pilgrimage*, Grant & Co. 1872

13   Besant, Walter, *London South of the Thames*, Adam & Charles Black 1912

14   *The Graphic*, 4th September 1920

15   Sinclair, Iain, *White Chappell Scarlet Tracings*, Vintage 1995

16   Sinclair, Iain, *Lud Heat* and *Suicide Bridge*, Vintage 1995

17   Southwark Borough Librarian, Letter to Mr MA Slee dated 7th May 1973, in Southwark Local Archives

18   Weeks, Margaret H. http://www.cryerfamilyhistory.co.uk/location-Horselydown.htm, 1972

THE LIBERTY OF NORTON FOLGATE

Norton Folgate was a place of distinct character, and its location adjacent to the City drew in marginal people, from actors to travellers to immigrants.

Introduction

It takes faith to believe Norton Folgate was, not long ago, a place in its own right. In its current incarnation it is simply a very short section of a long road, squeezed between Shoreditch and the City of London. Briefly, for 150 yards of its journey from London to East Anglia, the A10 becomes Norton Folgate. The surviving street name is a remnant, but Norton Folgate has history: it was once a liberty, independent of the local bishop and under the jurisdiction of St. Paul's Cathedral as early as the Domesday Book. Later the St. Mary Spital Priory and Hospital was built, covering most of its land. St. Mary Spital was demolished following the dissolution of the monasteries in the 1530s, but Norton Folgate remained as a shadow of the lost priory, the boundaries of the lost foundation preserved in a tiny, peculiar, self-governing knot of streets.

The Liberty of Norton Folgate lost its special status in 1900 when new Metropolitan Boroughs were created in London, excising anomalies and dividing the nine acres of the Liberty between Shoreditch and Stepney. During the centuries in between it enjoyed more than its share of the populous chaos and change that surged around the edge of the City. During its 350 years as a liberty, Norton Folgate was a place of distinct character, and its location adjacent to the City drew in marginal people, from actors to travellers to immigrants. The busy road was known for its taverns, fuelling the passers-by, and lined with small businesses, houses and the odd slaughterhouse. Behind the main street, Norton Folgate merged into Spitalfields which was built for Flemish Huguenot weavers who fled France in the 1680s, the first of several waves of new inhabitants to settle on the eastern edge of the City. All the while the tiny Liberty was overseen by its own council, known as the Ten Ancients.

In the 21st century Norton Folgate has become contested territory, an embattled buffer zone resisting and absorbing pressure as the City spills across its own ancient boundaries into neighbouring boroughs. It is divided between the City of London, and the Boroughs of Hackney and Tower Hamlets, the boundary line running down the middle of the main road. This frontline role has brought it minor cult status, linked to a revived interest in forgotten London. The Liberty now has its own independence campaign, provided the title for a Madness album[1] and currently has its own cafe, 'The Liberty of Norton Folgate', almost the last reminder that this street was once known for its inns and victuallers.

The Old North Road

Norton Folgate is the name for the section of main road connecting

Bishopsgate and Shoreditch High Street. Where Bishopsgate exits the City, the glass containers for banks, lawyers and insurers come to an abrupt halt and Norton Folgate begins, immediately a different territory with two-storey Victorian buildings, semi-abandoned low-rise warehouses and workshops, and a handful of sites that have been empty for years. This is an older London of pocket factories and tight alleyways, squeezed into a corner bounded by Commercial Street, the railway cuttings and bridges that run into Liverpool Street Station, and the City's new, glass walls.

By the time it was abolished in 1900, the former Liberty straddled the main road. The smaller western side covered what is now the area of the Broadgate Tower and Worship Street, while the bulk of its territory was to the east, from Fleur de Lis Street as far south as Spital Square, including the rebuilt western half of Spitalfields Market. These edges moved over time, and earlier maps show the boundary set further north along Hearn Street and Plough Yard.

Norton Folgate is part of the Old North Road, the Roman Ermine Street from London that crosses the flat country of Hertfordshire and Cambridgeshire en route to Lincoln and York. Its name implies a gate, but could equally refer to a Saxon word for a highway, or mean something like 'north farm'. There was a gate through the City walls, but it was further south: the Bishop's Gate, at the junction with Wormwood Street. The area beyond the gate was subsumed into the City, and its boundary is now halfway along Norton Folgate. Beyond Bishopsgate is Norton Folgate, "where the city bulges north."[2] It runs for 150 yards, coming to an end at a small but noticeable kink in the road which marks the line of the north wall of St. Mary Spital Priory and Hospital.

The first record of the nine acres of 'Norton Folyot' or 'Nortonfoly' manor is in 1442, in the records of the courts run by canons from St. Paul's Cathedral.[3] By the end of the 16th century "Norton Fall Gate, a Liberty so called"[4] was under the authority of the Dean of

St. Paul's, while the Lieutenant of the Tower of London commanded the military here and in several outlying districts around the east of the City. Norton Folgate had no village centre, with the lost St. Mary Spital leaving a space where its parish church should have been. Instead it revolved around the main road.

St. Mary Spital

The Augustinian Priory and Hospital of St. Mary without Bishopsgate, as St. Mary Spital was officially called, had its priory and main buildings at what is now Spital Square. It was founded around 1200 with land donated by a couple called Walter and Roisia Brunus. Spital is a shortened form of 'hospital' – medieval hospitals sheltered the poor and the sick – and the land outside the walls, the hospital fields, became shortened to Spitalfields.

The Priory was already in a poor state when the Dissolution came. In August 1538 the Lord Mayor of London, Sir Richard Gresham, reported to Thomas Cromwell that "the Rouffe and the Leedes and allssoo the Roodeloffte" of the church had collapsed.[5] The hospital was in a better state, and Gresham petitioned the King to hand over the three London hospitals of "Seynt Maryes Spytell, Seynt Bartholemews Spytell and Seint Thomas Spytell" to the Lord Mayor because he needed them to help the poor. John Stow described the hospital as "an Hospitall of great reliefe" containing "nine score beds well furnished for receipt of poore people." The Hospital, however, closed with the Priory and the small houses with gardens built there "for the decayed poor" fell into disrepair. Stow reported that "these Houses, for Want of Reparations, in few Years were so decayed, that it was called Rotten Row, and the poor worn out."[6] Barts and St. Thomas's began as medieval hospitals and have survived, sometimes against the odds, but St. Mary's is London's lost hospital. Another nearby foundation, the Priory of the New Order of St. Mary of Bethlem sited where Liverpool Street Station now stands, also survives as a

Derelict buildings, Norton Folgate

different type of hospital, known for many years as 'Bedlam' and now relocated to the fringes of London.

Excavations at Spital Square, on the site of the Priory graveyard, have revealed the remains of over 10,000 human skeletons buried there between the 12th and early 16th centuries. They include a mass burial of 4,000 people who died in the mid-13th century, recently linked to a huge eruption in around 1257 of an unknown volcano, possibly in Indonesia. The eruption is thought to have been eight times the size of the Krakatoa blast (also in Indonesia) in 1883, which led to five years of chaotic weather around the world. The debris thrown into the atmosphere in 1257 is thought to have caused the bitterly cold weather of that year and the failed crops recorded by writers in Britain at the time, which led to many deaths across the country.

The Old Artillery Ground

Places immediately beyond the City walls were often claimed for activity requiring extra space. While Norton Folgate became the grounds of St. Mary Spital, a complex that included the priory church and hospital buildings, a smaller area immediately to the south became a separate liberty, called the Old Artillery Ground. In the time of the Priory it was the 'Tesell Ground', perhaps named after the teasles planted there and used for brushing cloth. In 1537, just before the Priory was closed, the land was leased to "the Fraternyte or Guylde of Artyllary of Longebowes, Crossebowes and Handegonnes".[7]

Although the Guild relocated to Bunhill Fields in the 1640s, moving to the site still owned and used by the Honourable Artillery Company, gunnery continued in the Liberty. The Board of Ordnance, the government office that supplied armaments to the Army and Navy, was based at the Tower of London but stored gunpowder and tested weapons on what became known as the Artillery Ground. They also used another liberty for similar purposes: the Minories, immediately to the east of the Tower of London. The Master Gunner of England lived on site at the Artillery Ground, in a house near the north end of modern Steward Street. Samuel Pepys visited the Ground in 1669 and "by Captain Deane's invitation, did go to see his new gun tryed, this being the place where the Officers of the Ordnance do try all their great guns; and when we come, did find that the trial had been made; and they going away with extraordinary report of the proof of his gun, which, from the shortness and bigness, they do call Punchinello."[8]

Around the same time new houses began to crowd the walls of the Artillery Ground, and neighbours started to complain, particularly about the storage of large quantities of explosives. It became impractical to carry on testing guns in a rapidly urbanising area, and the Ordnance moved out in 1681. Houses were built on the Old Artillery Ground by developers who included the notorious Nicholas Barbon [see Wellclose: the Forgotten East End chapter], although the walls around the ground remained for many years afterwards. Today, the boundaries of the old liberty are equivalent to the modern Brushfield Street, Fort Street, Sandys Row, Artillery Row and Gun Street – names which reflect its former use – and cut across the middle of what is now Spitalfields Market. A street called Old Artillery Ground runs where the field once was.

Edge city

By the 1600s St. Mary Spital had been long abandoned although its buildings, like those of the nearby Holywell Priory in Shoreditch, were reused, adapted, and dismantled for stone. Norton Folgate however was a busy and eventful place. Traders of many types, both decent and dubious, could be found along the main road. Tailors, feltmakers and embroiderers prefigured the weavers who would arrive before the end of the century. Victuallers, butchers, chandlers, vinters, blacksmiths and even armourers catered to passing trade from those entering and leaving London.

While most were doubtless honest, in 1616 a gentlemen by the pleasing name of Walsingham Rippington was accused of "selling to victuallers strong drink and ale of extraordinary strength and price".[9] The illicit activities that found a home in the Liberty feature in court records. During the reign of Elizabeth I men were arrested for frequenting "suspected houses"[10] and a "notorious bawdy house"[11] in the Liberty, clearly an option available to those visiting Norton Folgate. In an incident straight from the plays of Ben Jonson, five men "cozened"[12] another of £6 at cards.

The time that the playwright Christopher Marlowe spent in Norton Folgate in the autumn of 1589 illustrates its location on the edge both geographically and socially, and provides a vivid picture of the men who lived there, many of whom seem to have carried swords as a matter of course. Marlowe, a literary genius at a young age, also seems to have been the original Cambridge spy. He was a

The Liberty of Norton Folgate Café, Norton Folgate

volatile and brilliant character who had worked for the Government since his university days in a capacity that could not be disclosed, and was eventually killed in a mysterious Deptford tavern fight aged only 29. However, even in 1589 Marlowe was living a dangerous life. It is not known when he arrived in London, but he presumably chose Norton Folgate because it was next to London's theatre district. At the time this consisted of only two establishments, The Theatre and The Curtain, outside the City Walls among the ruins of Holywell Priory off modern Curtain Road. Marlowe's plays will have been performed for the first time in these theatres.

The shadows obscuring the details of Marlowe's life are temporarily lifted by the court records of his part in a fatal street fight in Norton Folgate. On 18th September 1589 Marlowe was apparently attacked on Hog Lane (now Worship Street) by a man called William Bradley, who was involved in an unpleasant dispute over money owed to a man Marlowe knew. At a previous encounter Bradley and friends had clashed with Marlowe and his theatre friends and, according to Anthony Burgess's fictionalised account, "were surprised to find muscle under our gaudy onstage rainment."[13]

John Stow, writing not long afterwards, described Hog Lane as having recently "lost all pretensions to a rural or retired character". The fields on either side of Bishopsgate, he complained, had "been turned into Gardenplottes, teynter yardes, Bowling Allyes, and such like, from Houndes ditch in the West, so farre as white Chappell."[14]

When Marlowe was set upon in newly built-up Hog Lane, he drew his sword to defend himself and a friend, a poet called Thomas Watson, arrived on the scene. Too good a swordsman for Bradley, Watson killed him with a thrust to the heart. Both Marlowe and Watson were committed to Newgate Gaol on the orders of Stephen Wylde, a tailor and part-time Norton Folgate constable, while the death was investigated. Marlowe was released after only two weeks, but Watson spent five months behind bars before he was eventually acquitted of manslaughter. This was neither the last brawl to involve Marlowe, nor Norton Folgate. Well into the next century, it was still the kind of place where the watch would arrest a group of men for "going along "in a rantinge manner . . . .with bottles of sack in their hands."[15]

Sir Paul Pindar's Head

Bishopsgate and Norton Folgate were once known for their coaching inns, a number of which had yards surrounded by wooden galleries and were used for the performance of plays. The City's last galleried inn was the Catherine Wheel on Bishopsgate, 100 yards south of Norton Folgate, which was demolished in 1911. A melancholy passageway, Catherine Wheel Alley, marks the site.

However, the most famous of these inns is, bizarrely, hanging on a wall at the Victoria and Albert Museum. When the Sir Paul Pindar's Head tavern was demolished in 1890 for the construction of Liverpool Street Station its fine 1599 'jettied' wooden façade was donated to the V&A and is now on display, a frontage without a building, resembling the discarded exo-skeleton of some ancient London mollusc.

The tavern was originally part of a mansion built by Sir Paul Pindar, an impressively bearded diplomat and merchant who did very well under James I but had the misfortune to lend large amounts of money to Charles I, who did not pay him back. Pindar died in financial difficulties, but his house outlived him by two and half centuries: surviving the Great Fire of London, becoming successively the Venetian Ambassador's residence, a workhouse, apartments and finally a tavern. By the time it was demolished it was part of a row of narrow three-storey houses with businesses on the ground floors: a piano factory to one side of the tavern and William Sorrell's Coffee Rooms on the other.

Weaver's Town
Piecemeal development around the Priory walls, and eventually of the Priory grounds themselves, created the tangle of streets and alleys that still characterise Norton Folgate and Spitalfields. There was also enough land for larger developments that still stand, including the Truman Brewery on Brick Lane which opened in 1669, and Spitalfields Market which was granted a charter in 1682. However, the area really began to change after Protestant rights were suppressed in France with the revocation of the Edict of Nantes in 1685, bringing large numbers of Huguenot (French Protestant) refugees to London. Many were silk weavers, and there had been French weavers in Spitalfields for several years before the refugee influx, with tensions between native apprentices and immigrant weavers reported as early as 1683. By 1700 the Huguenots were firmly established, with nine churches and a soup kitchen for the poor (called La Soupe).

In the 1680s construction began on Spital Square, with large houses designed for the men at the top of the local trade – master weavers and silk merchants. The silk weavers and journeymen lived in lesser accommodation, in the alleys and back streets still to be found behind the formal streets, of which Elder and Folgate Streets are the best examples in Norton Folgate. Some houses have long weavers' windows on the upper storey, to provide light for working. By around 1740, the area between Norton Folgate and Brick Lane had been completely built over, creating modern Spitalfields.

Dennis Severs' House at 18 Folgate Street, with a weaver's bobbin sign hanging outside, is typical of the respectable homes built in Spitalfields at the time. Severs moved into the dilapidated 1724 house in 1978, and gradually turned it into a museum that tells the history of the area through aura and atmosphere rather than information, beginning with traces of St. Mary Spital recreated in the basement. It also serves as a monument to 1970s Spitalfields when Severs, who died in 1999, moved there. Many of the 17th and 18th century buildings were in poor repair and the area was still a working market quarter, where groups of rough sleepers would gather round fires in winter and scavenge leftover vegetables from the market. Severs was one of a number of artists, architectural historians and Spitalfields enthusiasts who restored the weavers' houses, including matching artists Gilbert and George. Since then Spitalfields has risen inexorably in the world, with houses expensively refurbished and then offices inevitably moving in. In the course of its reinvention it has come to completely overshadow Norton Folgate, and no-one visiting Dennis Severs' house would know it is not in fact in Spitalfields.

The wealth of the most successful silk merchants was reflected in the grandeur of their houses but Weavers' Town, as the newly built area became known, was always a mixture of wealth and poverty. Master weavers employed groups of journeymen, skilled and unskilled, and lived alongside them. In the 1730s Irish weavers began to arrive, working alongside the Huguenot immigrants, although not always harmoniously. The neighbourhood was volatile, attributed by a writer of the 1930s to "an excitability" characteristic of the Huguenots' "foreign origin".[16] When printed calico began to arrive from India in the early 1700s, undercutting London prices, weavers were reported to have torn calico dresses from women in the street. Tensions grew over French imports and pay for journeymen in the 1760s. Illegal unions were formed, and employers who undercut pay demands might find their silk slashed. Wars with France ended in 1763, leading to competition, and in 1765 weavers besieged Parliament during the debate on an import bill, committing "divers Insolencies and Outrages to the Peers who passed to and from this House, so that some of them were in imminent Danger of their Lives."[17] Matters came to a head after several years of violence in 1769, when soldiers fired on a group of silk cutters outside the Dolphin pub (off Artillery Lane) and killed two men. Two more were later hung, on dubious evidence.

The Spitalfields Act, introduced in 1778, equalised wages for the same quantities of work and was intended to prevent disputes. It created a bizarre system in which magistrates would count the threads in a square inch of silk to ensure weavers were paid fairly. This did the trade no favours, and it began to move away to other parts of the country. In 1831, though, there were still as many as 17,000 looms in Spitalfields and Norton Folgate, and 50,000 people dependent on them. However, by the end of the 19th century all the silk firms had moved out, many to Braintree in Essex which became a weaving centre in its own right.

Road and rail

By the 1890s Norton Folgate was a changed place, more like its current incarnation. Commercial Road had been cut through in 1840, creating a new eastern boundary for the neighbourhood. In the 1860s and 1870s, new railway lines created boundaries to the north and west, crossing Norton Folgate at the junction with Shoreditch High Street, and eliminating networks of lanes and alleys to the west of Norton Folgate. The Bishopsgate Goods Station, built on the northern edge of Norton Folgate in 1840, was destroyed in a huge fire in 1964. Shoreditch Station now occupies part of the site, surrounded by the wasteland strip that separates Norton Folgate from Shoreditch.

Liverpool Street Station opened in 1874 on the site of the original Royal Bethlem Hospital or 'Bedlam', which had moved to Moorfields in 1676. Broad Street Station next door was built on the Bethlehem Churchyard, which contained the bodies of those from Bedlam and many others besides. When the station was demolished to build the Broadgate Centre, 400 skeletons were uncovered, and several hundred more came to light during works to build the Crossrail station.

Liverpool Street Station, extensively rebuilt and reopened in 1992, is greatly changed from the Victorian original which by all accounts was dark and unsettling. W.G. Sebald, unable to see it as anything other than the British terminus for the Kindertransport route by which Jewish children escaped Nazi Germany, wrote: "Before work began to rebuild it at the end of the 1980s this station, with its main concourse fifteen to twenty feet below street level, was one of the darkest and most sinister places in London, a kind of entrance to the underworld, as it has often been described."[18]

The station has attracted a certain amount of misfortune. It was hit during the first major bombing raid of the First World War, with 162 people killed. Field Marshal Sir Henry Williams unveiled a memorial in 1922 to those who died, and was murdered by IRA gunmen on his return home from the ceremony. The 1993 Provisional IRA Bishopsgate bomb also damaged the station, and one of the 7th July 2005 attackers exploded a bomb on a Circle Line train as it left Liverpool Street, heading for Aldgate.

The Abyss

By the end of the 19th century the East End was horrifically, notoriously overcrowded and poverty stricken. In 1902 the author Jack London lived in Spitalfields and Whitechapel for several months to research his book, *People of the Abyss*. Unafraid of sensationalism, he first dropped in at Thomas Cook & Son on Cheapside to inform them of his plans, saying "I wish you to understand in advance what I intend doing, so that in case of trouble you may be able to identify me." The assistant, allegedly, replied: "Ah, I see! Should you be murdered, we would be in position to identify the corpse."[19]

He wrote that "in the shadow of Christ's Church, at three o'clock in the afternoon, I saw a sight I never wish to see again. A chill, raw wind was blowing… here were a dozen women, ranging in age from twenty years to seventy. Next a babe, possibly of nine months, lying asleep, flat on the hard bench, with neither pillow nor covering, nor with any one looking after it. Next half-a-dozen men, sleeping bolt upright or leaning against one another in their sleep." The homeless were forbidden to lie down to sleep outside. London described the East End as "an abscess, a great putrescent sore."[20] Not long before, Israel Zangwill had described Fashion Street, next to Christchurch Spitalfields, as "'Rotten Row'… within earshot of the blasphemies from some of the vilest quarters and filthiest rookeries in the capital of the civilised world."[21] His phraseology unconsciously echoed John Stow's description of the area, 300 years earlier.

Streets in Spitalfields, within a stone's throw of Norton Folgate, became known as the worst in London, especially Dorset Street with its "thieves, prostitutes and bullies"[22] where Jack the Ripper's final victim, Mary Jane Kelly, was found eviscerated in a back room. Commercial Road, behind Norton Folgate, also had a bad reputation, confirmed by incidents such as the stabbing to death of a policeman in 1900 as he attempted to disperse a group of men gathered around a coffee stall.

Newspapers frequently linked events such as these to immigration, reporting after this particular murder that "in this district English people are the exceptions, Germans, Poles, and Russians the rule. The flashing eyes and crisp black hair of the men and women one meets on the pavements suggest rather an Eastern city than London."[23] This widespread paranoia resulted from the arrival of large numbers of Ashkenazi Jews, who began leaving Russia for Britain after the famine of 1869-70, peaking with pogroms in Russian and Prussia in the 1880s and 1890s. The Alien Immigration Act of 1905 ended the influx, in reaction to public disquiet. However, Norton Folgate and Spitalfields remained distinctively Jewish areas for nearly a century.

At the turn of the century, Norton Folgate had a mixture of Irish and Jewish inhabitants, and poverty next door to respectable working class streets. The northern part of Norton Folgate was more Irish, with Spitalfields market porters and labourers living in places such as Fleur de Lis Street. Tailors and bootmakers lived on Blossom Street, "Respectable tradesmen, workshops, furriers, Jews" on Elder Street. Further south, the streets were less well-to-do, with Wheeler Street having "several ticket of leave men living here, mess on st bread, paper, old boots, windows broken".[24] On Artillery Court, social researcher Charles Booth reported "a queue for the doss house three hours before it opened." Little Pearl Street was "a thoroughly vicious quarter. The Cambridge Music Hall in Commercial Street makes it a focussing point for prostitutes".[25]

Norton Folgate was part of a market quarter, which spread well beyond Spitalfields Market. A list of the markets reads like an elegy for the lost East End:

"The Brick Lane Market, the Wentworth Street Market (every day but Saturday), the Watney Street Market, the Salmon Lane Market, the Cambridge Road Market, the Coulston Street Market, the Middlesex Street (Sunday morning) market, the Hessel Street Market, the Sclater Street and Club Row bird and dog market (Sunday morning), the

Fleur de Lis Street, Spitalfields

Aldgate (South side) market, the White Horse Street and Durham
Row markets, and the Mile End Waste (Saturday) Market. Most of
these are pure London, but the Brick Lane and Wentworth Street
markets are largely Jewish and Russian. There are also the wholesale
market of Spitalfields, for fruit and vegetables, and the Whitechapel
Hay Market."[26]

The Jewish East End, at its height between the wars, was a shabby
but vibrant place, overcrowded but filled with traders and residents
inhabiting a maelstrom of activity. It was "a hard-working district of
sinewy cabinet-makers, round-shouldered tailors, itinerant street
vendors hoarsely praising the goods on their barrows, furriers, button-
hole makers, housewives battling the daily grime that seeps in from
the littered pavements… People spoke of Warsaw, Kishinev, Kiev,
Kharkov, Odessa as if they were neighbouring suburbs".[27]

Shops on Norton Folgate itself were Jewish-run by the 1890s. Arthur Morrison's *A Child of the Jago* describes "a shop of cheap second-hand miscellanies: saddles, razors, straps, dumbbells, pistols, boxing gloves, trunks, bags, and billiard-balls. Many of the things hung about the door-posts in bunches, and within all was black, as in a cave. At one door-post was a pistol."[28]

Norton Folgate however still catered to the many people who passed through: "On the west side are public houses of all kinds… the haunt of carmen, good 'pull-ups' and large modern with grill room and luncheon room for the city man and clerk."

The Ancients

The abolition of the Liberty in 1900 also saw the end of Norton Folgate's peculiar system of local government. The Liberty had secular governance from at least the 1650s rather than being run by the church, as was the case in other London liberties. Ten "ancient inhabitants" formed a local council chaired by the Headborough (whose title describes his job), a leftover from the Saxon system of local government and law enforcement. There were four other officers of the Liberty: two overseers who collected rents; a scavenger who cleaned the streets; and a constable.

The system was reformed in the early 1800s, when the ten Ancients were replaced by a board of 20 Trustees. The Ancients, and later the Trustees of the Liberty of Norton Folgate, met in the Norton Folgate Court House which from 1744 was at No.1 Folgate Street. The last meeting here was held on 24th October 1900, although the building lasted until 1965. Relics from Norton Folgate's civic past also survive, buried in the Tower Hamlets archives. Three beadle's rods, symbols of authority for the Norton Folgate constable, and a box for collecting alms are preserved. The rods are a particularly poignant reminder of the tiny, vanished Liberty: one, from the coronation of George IV in 1821, is topped with a miniature four-bar gate, a symbol punning on its name.

Norton Folgate has stood increasingly in the way of progress since the 19th century expansion of London, and remarkably enough it retains some of the character of a shabby frontier with the City of London. However, in many ways it is a commercial City neighbourhood, with a population of only around 200 people in contrast to the 1,600 who lived there in 1901. In 1894 a cockney character in a George Bernard Shaw play could still say "Well, I never met a man as didn't know Nortn Folgit before!"[29] as a piece of one-upmanship.

Yet the neighbourhood has not yet succumbed entirely to City takeover bids. Intense battles have been fought during the last ten years over the construction of new offices. On the west side of Norton Folgate, glass walls have marched up Bishopsgate to the boundary with Hackney, at Primrose Street, the very edge of Norton Folgate. On the east side of the road they have breached the lines and broken into Tower Hamlets, with the redevelopment of Spitalfields Market.

Remarkably, Norton Folgate is still noticeably a separate place from the neighbouring City of London, hovering just beyond its reach. Change is coming though, slowly but remorselessly. The remaining stretch of low-rise 18th and 19th century shops and houses, at Nos. 13-20 on the eastern side of Norton Folgate, has been boarded up since an application to demolish them was turned down in 2008. Blossom Place, behind the terraces and the Arts and Crafts Water Poet pub, backs onto surviving wash houses with their own chimneys and water towers, the subject of English Heritage objections. The Nicholls and Clarke building, a 1930s tile showroom and yard, adjoins Norton Folgate where the A10 becomes Shoreditch High Street. It has been empty since 2003, but a planning application for the site was approved in 2011. Although unseen for centuries, the Priory of St. Mary Spital makes its presence felt in Norton Folgate, its archaeology still complicating building works.

A long-running application for a tower on empty land north

Blossom Street, Spitalfields

of Primrose Street originally involved demolishing the Light Bar, housed in a former Great Eastern Railway electricity sub-station. A campaign persuaded Hackney Council to turn the plans down, with tactics that included challenging the legality of the Liberty of Norton Folgate's 1900 abolition. Campaigners supposedly planned to declare independence, adding to a rich tradition of London neighbourhoods that fight back, from *Passport to Pimlico* to short-lived enclaves such as Frestonia in Notting Dale, which tried to secede in 1977. A group calling itself the Liberty of Norton Folgate Community Council[30] keeps the idea of self-government alive.

Nowhere better illustrates the transition of the national economy in the last 30 years, from production to services sold from offices, than Norton Folgate. It is both a physical and an economic frontier, visibly separating the new economy from the old. The shift from one era to the next is being acted out in a struggle to control the absurdly valuable land of the Liberty, hugged by the City in a terminal embrace.

REFERENCES

1   Madness, *The Liberty of Norton Folgate* (2009)

2   Sebald, W.G. *Austerlitz*, Penguin 2002

3   Sheppard, F.H.W. *Survey of London: Volume 27: Spitalfields and Mile End New Town*, Athlone Press for the London County Council 1957

4   Stow, John, *The Survey of London*, Everyman 1912

5   Sheppard, F.H.W. *Survey of London: Volume 27: Spitalfields and Mile End New Town*, Athlone Press for the London County Council 1957

6   *ibid*

7   Sheppard, F.H.W. *Survey of London: Volume 27: Spitalfields and Mile End New Town*, Athlone Press for the London County Council 1957

8   Pepys, Samuel, *The Diary of Samuel Pepys* Vol. 9 1668-9. University of California Press 1995

9   'Sessions, 1616: 11 and 12 January', County of Middlesex. Calendar to the sessions records: new series, volume 3: 1615-16 (1937)

10   'Middlesex Sessions Rolls: 1589', Middlesex County Records: Volume 1: 1550-1603 (1886)

11   'Sessions, 1614: 3 and 5 December', County of Middlesex. Calendar to the sessions records: new series, volume 2: 1614-15 (1936)

12   'Sessions, 1616: 17 and 20 February', County of Middlesex. Calendar to the sessions records: new series, volume 3: 1615-16 (1937)

13   Burgess, Anthony, *A Dead Man in Deptford*, Vintage 1994

14   A Survey of London, by John Stow: Reprinted from the text of 1603 (1908)

15   Middlesex County Records: Volume 3: 1625-67 (1888)

16   Maddocks, Sydney, 'Spitalfields' in *The Copartnership Herald*, Vol. II, no. 13 (March 1932)

17   *Journal of the House of Lords volume 31: 1765-1767*, History of Parliament Trust, (1767-1830)

18   Sebald, W.G. *Austerlitz*, Penguin 2002

19   London, Jack, *People of the Abyss*, The Echo Library 2007

20   *ibid*

21   Zangwill, Israel, *Children of the Ghetto*, W. Heinemann 1893

22   Booth, Charles, *Survey Into Life and Labour in London 1886-1903*, LSE Charles Booth Online Archive

23   *News Of The World*, Sunday, 2nd December, 1900

24   Booth, Charles, *Survey Into Life and Labour in London 1886-1903*, LSE Charles Booth Online Archive

25   *ibid*

26   Burke, Thomas & Binder, Pearl, *The Real East End*, Constable & Co. Ltd. 1932

27   Litvinoff, Emanuel, 'A Jew in England' in *Journey Through A Small Planet*, Penguin 2008

28   Morrison, Arthur, *A Child of the Jago*, Methuen & Co. 1896

29   Shaw, George Bernard, 'Candida', *Plays Pleasant*, Penguin Classics 2003

30   http://www.norton-folgate.co.uk, accessed 8th February 2013

LIMEHOUSE: LONDON'S FIRST CHINATOWN

*From the late 19th century until the Second
World War, Limehouse was synonymous
with poverty, crime, drugs, violence and,
above all, foreigners.*

Introduction

Limehouse is a natural, sheltered landing place hidden in the crook
of the extravagant Thames loop around the Isle of Dogs. Although
the inner London docks are long closed, it is still a riverside
neighbourhood. Its spine is Narrow Street, curled tightly against the
river; narrowed by the former wharves and warehouse, squeezed
on to small plots jostling for river frontage. Behind Narrow Street is
Limehouse Basin, lined with pleasure boats. It is the meeting point
for the Thames, the Regent's Canal and the Limehouse Cut, which
links Limehouse to London's eastern artery at the River Lea. The still-
strange Isle of Dogs is next door, an isolated marsh peninsula hollowed

out for the huge basins of the West India and Millwall Docks. But between the canals and the docks a patch of streets, concealed at the unvisited end of Limehouse, boasts curiously Chinese names. These were once Chinatown, the most mythologised place in London.

London's Chinatown is now so firmly established between Leicester Square and Shaftesbury Avenue that an alternative is hard to imagine. But before Gerrard Street, London's first Chinatown was a place of fear, fascination and wild stories. From the late 19th century until the Second World War, Limehouse was synonymous with poverty, crime, drugs, violence and, above all, foreigners. Its malign influence supposedly reached into respectable London, luring and corrupting the innocent. The most famous writers and film-makers of the age, who queued up to tell stories of mysterious Eastern corruption and terror, all centred on a few Limehouse streets. Not quite everything was fantasy, but the difference between the Chinatown myth and the real Limehouse tells us much about London at the peak of its imperial power.

Today, the buildings that made up this semi-real place have been completely erased, but the street pattern has not. Much of the East End feels haunted, but this is particularly so along the East India Dock Road through Limehouse where the faded present is a hollow echo of the past. In the heart of this absent place, the Chinatown streets are a complex and curious place, still waiting to be discovered, possibly for the first time.

Lime and luxury goods

Limehouse is named after the oast houses – kilns used to make quicklime for mortar – set up here from the 14th century onwards. The downwind fields to the east of the City provided a convenient place for the 'obnoxious industries' servicing London's building needs. As river trade grew in the 1600s London came to meet Limehouse, which had been connected to the City only by a string of buildings along the river. The East End villages along the Thames – Limehouse, Ratcliff and Wapping – were the home ports for London's merchant shipping. They supplied accommodation, provisions and chandlery, including ship's rope which was made on the long rope walks which dominated the Limehouse area, memorialised in Ropemaker's Fields at the eastern end of Narrow Street.

By the start of the 18th century, Limehouse consisted of houses grouped around Church Lane (now Newell Street) and Three Colt Street, and a series of wharves along the Thames shore. It was still in many ways a country village, with the parish records noting arguments over the amount of punch and wine charged to the parish by churchwardens, and a Parish Commission featuring names from Thomas Hardy's discard pile, including Mr Crotchrode Whiffing. However, the parish burial registers from the 1730s and 1740s include two Venetians, two West Indians, a Dane and a Lascar (an Indian), showing that Limehouse was no ordinary parish, already linked far and wide by sea.

The opening of the Limehouse Cut in 1770 introduced a new era, as purpose-built, industrialised docks replaced the river wharves. New basins, canals and enclosed docks, dug to shelter larger ships, punched Limehouse full of holes. The West India Docks, opened in 1802, were on a leviathan scale different to anything seen before. Three enclosed basins covered more than 70 acres, surrounded by a 20-foot brick wall to keep pilferers out. Valuable Jamaican coffee, sugar, rum, mahogany and teak, arriving from West Indies plantations, was stored in warehouses five storeys high which stretched for half a mile.

The three West India Dock basins – the Import, Export and South Docks – were partly decked over with concrete for the construction of Canary Wharf, but long stretches remain intact. The Docks, which consumed 6,000 tons of Dorking limestone and 24 million bricks, were designed with 'banana' walls with a curved profile to help the bulging hulls of ships slip by. New roads were built to link the Docks to the City, with the Commercial Road and East India Dock Road defining a new northern boundary for Limehouse, while the West India Dock Road carved unceremoniously through its middle. West India Docks Station, on a site at the junction of West India Dock Road and Hertsmere Road, closed in 1926, although the Docklands Light Railway at Shadwell now uses its viaduct.

The new super-sized docks brought unprecedented numbers of men (but virtually no women) to Limehouse from all over the globe, working the ships and the quays. In 1818, a group of seven men charged with sleeping rough in a Limehouse brickfield proved to be, variously, from Antigua, Corsica, Gloucestershire, Jamaica, Portugal, Wapping and Whitehaven. When the East and West India Companies merged in 1838 the West India Docks and the East India Docks at Blackwall, on the opposite side of the Isle of Dogs, became a single operation. Their imports of spices, tea and wine from the Orient were added to the mix, bringing in many more sailors from the East, and inaugurating a century of huge change for Limehouse. As a later author commented "To thousands and thousands of foreigners, London means the West India Dock Road and nothing more".[1]

The Opium Connection

The history of the Chinese in Britain seems to have begun in 1686 with the first recorded Chinese visitor, a young man called Michael Alphonsius Shen Fu-Tsung. Having converted to Christianity and become a Jesuit in China, he was presented to James II by a Jesuit missionary as part of a European tour. Sir Godfrey Kneller painted his portrait, 'The Chinese Convert', which was hung in the King's bed-chamber. He also visited the Bodleian Library in Oxford, where he allegedly showed the librarians which way up to hold their collection of Chinese books.

However, Shen Fu-Tsung aside, it was the British East India Company, commercial behemoth of the British Empire and ruler of

Chun Yee Society, East India Dock Road

India until 1857, which first brought Chinese people to Britain. Trade between Britain and China began in the 1600s, with the company's ships importing tea, silks and ceramics. Asian sailors arrived with the ships and at first lodged in Shadwell, immediately west of Limehouse. In 1805 'John Anthony', the East India Company's accommodation fixer for Chinese sailors in East London, was the first Chinese man to take British citizenship. His naturalisation required a special Act of Parliament.

Trade between Britain and China was mainly conducted with the city of Canton (now Guangzhou) on the Pearl River delta. However, the East India Company – known colloquially as 'John Company' – used shamelessly aggressive tactics to open up new trade. It was the primary instigator of the two Opium Wars (1839-42 and 1856-60) with China. Anglo-Indian and Anglo-French forces defeated the attempts of China's Qing Dynasty rulers to prevent John Company importing opium from its huge factories in India. The wars forcibly opened up trade with China, and established 'treaty ports' with trade concessions to Western powers, as well as ceding Hong Kong to the British on a long lease. This was the start of what the Chinese Communist Party later labelled the 'century of humiliation'.

Opium is the link between Canton and Limehouse, a sweet, sickly intoxicant that crossed the world and brought the East into London's backyards and on to its front pages. The opium trade was vast and lucrative, estimated as the most valuable trade of the mid-19th century in any single commodity. John Company ran poppy plantations in Bengal and factories in Benares (now Varanasi) and Patna, their warehouses stacked 50 feet high with opium balls wrapped in protective poppy petals. With the arrival of larger, more powerful steam ships and the opening of the Suez Canal in 1869, trade routes to China expanded further and more sailors than ever worked on ships plying between London and China, arriving at the East and West India Docks.

The streets of Limehouse

The modern map of Limehouse features a cluster of streets with Chinese names, either side of the East India Dock Road. Near Westferry station Amoy Place and Ming Street stand out from the solidly English names around them. Ming Street was in fact King Street until 1938, its name changed in a neat concession to its Chinese residents. Before post-war reconstruction there was also an Oriental Street, its site now somewhere under the Birchfield Street council blocks. On the north side of the East India Dock Road are Canton Street and Pekin Street. Canton Street dates back to 1868 and there was a Pekin Street then too, but in a different place to the current version, on a site now covered by Gladstone House.

However, the two streets synonymous with Chinatown were Limehouse Causeway and Pennyfields – less exotic sounding, but once universally known. Both streets were bywords for an entire world of strange, degenerate, foreign doings that existed, for the most part, in the imagination rather than in Limehouse.

The 'Penny Field' was developed with tenements and cottages in the mid-1600s, during the earliest throes of Limehouse's transformation from village to city. By the mid-1800s it was becoming a maritime neighbourhood, with King Street home to the workshops and warehouses of chandlers, joiners, riggers, ropemakers, sailmakers and more. The expansion of the Docks in the mid-1800s created a place that mixed Scandinavian sailors, Irish dock workers, German tailors, shoemakers, and bakers.

The Chinese and Lascar sailors arriving in larger numbers from the 1860s were mostly transient, coming and going with their ships. The 1881 census shows only 224 Chinese living in the whole of Britain, although more were doubtless unrecorded. It was not until the 1890s that a permanent Chinese population, probably around 300 people, became established in Limehouse, based at first on Limehouse Causeway. Initially, the sailors settling on the Causeway were Cantonese, from the opium port of Canton. Later, Chinatown expanded east along Pennyfields and along a few of the surrounding streets, where immigrants from Shanghai set up an adjacent but distinct trading community.

The Real Chinatown

Sailors who settled in London were exclusively male, but a number married English women and had families. After the First World War there was a lull in the growth of the Chinese population, large numbers of Chinese sailors and labourers having left to take part in the war effort. In 1918 only 182 Chinese were recorded as living in Limehouse, nine of whom were married to English women. The

Saunders Close, Limehouse Causeway

actual size of Chinatown is in remarkable contrast to its reputation,
which soon grew out of proportion to any reality.

Chinatown provided facilities for the Chinese sailors who passed
through: Chinese associations, eating houses, groceries, laundries and
lodging houses, catering to the needs of men who would leave again
on the next ship that would employ them. Like any port there were
also brothels in Limehouse, and sailors brought the habit of opium
smoking with them from China. Opium was legal in Britain, along
with the full array of now-prohibited drugs, until 1914. During the
second half of the 19th century a pipe of opium was considerably
cheaper than a pint of beer.

Social surveyor Charles Booth visited Limehouse Causeway in
the 1890s,[2] and called at an opium den. The policeman showing
him around helpfully explained how "Chinamen are very slippery,

tricky and cunning". He found two Chinese men lying on a low bed, smoking opium, whom he described as "A happy, jolly looking Chinaman, wreathed in smiles, who had smoked" and "a very sour looking pig-tailed heathen who was just starting his pipe." There was "a great ticking of clocks – there were seven lying all about the room – so that the men may see when to get back to their ships." Opium was only part of the owner's business: he also recruited Chinese crews for ships, and ran a general store for sailors.

Booth also visited a second opium den just outside Limehouse, on Jamaica Road in Stepney, which was run by an educated woman "who had seen better things" and her Indian husband. She indulged in a spot of 'mother's little helper', telling Booth "I feel all dribs and drabs, and cannot do any of my housework before my smoke in the morning." Her customers were sailors, including Chinese and Lascars, who apparently preferred to smoke in the mornings as they had to be back on their ships by 7pm. Charmingly, the payment system was an honesty box.

Limehouse, like most of the Docks neighbourhoods, combined the respectable with the squalid. Gill Street, Jamaica Place and Rich Street, both immediately off Limehouse Causeway, were streets of ill-repute, according to Booth: "a nest of brothels frequented by common seamen of every nationality. Twenty of the 24 houses in Jamaica Place were brothels. The same was the case in Rich Street. The business is profitable. There's a lot of money to be made by robbing the sailors."[3] Jamaica Place had in fact just had a name change to Beccles Street (its current name) "in the hope that a new name may help it in achieving a new character. It has not done so." He also identified the district as "a hotbed of venereal disease" and rated Chusan Street, off Commercial Road, as the heart of the criminal East End: "This is one of the blackest spots in London. 'I don't expect you will find it on your map, practically only the police know of its existence'" commented his police escort.[4]

The streets in which the Chinese settled were next door, but more respectable. Chinese businesses brought in regular incomes so, while sailors came and went, those who remained in London were able to establish themselves. When Booth visited, Evans Street had just changed its name to Pekin Street and was desirable enough to have police officers living on it. Pennyfields was "Respectable on the north side. South side many boarding houses for foreign seamen and one or two noted brothels." There was very little happening there – just two pubs and four small shops, one of which sold horsemeat for cats. Booth reflected on the nature of Chinese men in London: "He tries to be like an Englishman. When he comes to London he drinks beer, gets drunk and runs after women." He also discussed Japanese immigrants in a way that suggested there were as many as there were Chinese. It may be that popular accounts failed to make the distinction between China and Japan, but the Japanese have failed to find a place in the Limehouse myth.

A variety of clubs and organisations set up to help Chinese seamen was established in Limehouse around the turn of the 20th century, of which the best known was probably the Chinese Mission House on West India Dock Road, run by Rev. George Piercy who had spent 30 years as a missionary in China. Opposite was the Stranger's Home for Asiatics, opened in 1856 by Prince Albert, and later known as the Overseas Home. Neither survive, but The Sailor's Mission Hall building still dominates Commercial Road. Formerly the Empire Memorial Sailors' Hall, it was built in 1924 to serve sailors of all origins. Disused by 1960, it provided an ideally obscure venue for the Fourth Situationist International conference in 1960 and was a homeless hostel for many years, before conversion into flats.

The Yellow Peril

Relations between China and the West were volatile at the start of the 20th century, with China forced to trade against its will and France,

Germany, Japan and Russia all carving out areas of influence in the country. In 1901 an Eight-Nation Alliance including Britain sent troops into Peking to crush an anti-Western uprising. Droughts followed by floods and famine had exacerbated tensions with colonial occupiers in China, particularly as represented by Christian missionaries. The Righteous Harmony Society, a group of mainly dispossessed Chinese also known as 'The Boxers', grew in size and influence. Using martial arts, sabotage and frenzied 'spirit soldiers' they besieged the Western legations in Peking, but were defeated by international forces. US troops scaled the walls of the Imperial City, and the British Navy arrived to relieve the siege.

The Boxer Rebellion whipped up hysteria and a lust for revenge in the West. *The Times* reported in detail, entirely untruthfully as it turned out, that "a moving swarm" of Boxers had broken into the British Embassy in Peking and slaughtered everyone there, including "the helpless women and children".[5] *The New York Times* claimed Boxers had cut off the heads of their victims and paraded them through the streets on their rifles. None of these things had actually happened, but that did not prevent the self-righteous anger from escalating. The concept of the 'Yellow Peril', the threat from the East, took root in British culture where it remained embedded until the Second World War. In particular the novel *The Yellow Danger* by M.P. Shiel, published in 1898, peddled scare stories about the rise of the East, claiming that Britain "lies open to the locust swarm of the yellow race."[6]

The scare was revived during the 1906 election campaign, which featured both Labour and Liberals campaigning against the use of cheap Chinese labour in South Africa, and of Chinese crews on British ships, displacing British sailors. Dockers in Liverpool dressed in Chinese costumes, which "the angry cry of 'Pigtail' echoed through the constituencies… with virulence equal to its irrelevance".[7] Soon afterwards *The East End News* published letters repeatedly complaining about the Chinese in Limehouse, accusing them of letting off fireworks, spitting in the street, failing to observe the Sabbath, and attacking each other with choppers, added to which "the smell is almost torture"[8] – of what, they did not explain.

The Chinese inhabitants of Limehouse were concentrated in a few streets, no doubt encouraged to live close together by latent hostility that occasionally boiled over. In 1908 there were violent clashes at the Board of Trade Offices on East India Dock Road, where British sailors prevented Chinese from signing on for work, and their concerns about the number of Chinese seamen on British ships were supported by Winston Churchill. In 1911 all 33 Chinese laundries in Cardiff were attacked by rioters. More protests were organised against Chinese sailors in Limehouse in 1916. Race riots occurred in several cities in May and June 1919, including attacks on Chinese people and premises in Limehouse.

There was a general belief that while the British had been away fighting, the Chinese had taken their jobs. In Limehouse, tensions were stoked by provocative press reports of which this from the *Daily Express* is a good example: "Turn down Burdett Road into the West India Dock Road. That is the way to the narrow, dirty streets where San Sing squats on the pavement of a night, smoking his long pipe and blinking up at the moon through its smoke... Chinatown is growing. There are more Chinese in the purlieus of Rock Street and Pennyfields than ever before. The shop signs are creeping west."[9] There were greatly exaggerated claims from the police and from unions that 8,000 Chinese lived in Limehouse.

The theme of war between East and West featured in popular fiction, including H.G. Wells' *The War in the Air* (1907). Jack London's 1910 novel, *The Unparalleled Invasion*, is a fantasy of future Chinese dominance of the West. Eventual Western victory is achieved via mass genocide using biological weapons.

The myths around Chinatown grew uncontrollably. Chinese novelist Lao She wrote in 1929 that "If there were 20 Chinese living in Chinatown, their accounts would say five thousand; moreover every one of these five thousand yellow devils would certainly smoke opium, smuggle arms, murder people then stuff the corpses under beds, and rape women regardless of age…"[10]

From the pages of Dickens

The Mystery of Edwin Drood, Charles Dickens' final, unfinished novel, published in 1870, opens in an East End opium den. This scene is the first literary representation of the Chinatown myth, although Dickens had previously included an opium overdose in *Bleak House,* a theme also taken up by Gothic novelist Sheridan LeFanu in *Uncle Silas* around the same time. Sinister choirmaster John Jasper, an opium addict, experiences a drug-induced vision in which an English cathedral morphs into a spike, on which a Sultan impales Turkish robbers. Dickens' image captures the combination of terror and fascination that the fabled terrors of the East could be found in the very heart of the capital.

Dickens is thought to have based his account on a visit to an opium den in Bluegate Fields, an alley off Ratcliff Highway, and the distinctive opium pipe he describes, made from an inkwell, seems to have been based on an actual pipe. In the 1860s there were said to be three premises in the alley where opium could be smoked, while another two operated in Limehouse. The keeper of the Bluegate Fields opium house, Chi Ki, even hosted a visit from the Prince of Wales (later Edward VII), saying "I was sorry that the place was in such a muddle; but the Prince didn't seem to mind."[11]

Gustav Doré's engravings of the East End for Blanchard Jerrold's *London: A Pilgrimage* published in 1872, are all gothic shadows, seething poverty and crowds of skeletal children, and follow smoothly on from his phantasmagorical illustrations for Dante's *Inferno*. One plate in particular sums up the Limehouse of the imagination: an Asian sailor reclines on a bed with a long opium pipe, his face lit by the glow

Derelict site, West India Dock Road

of the lamp he is using to light it. He has a strange grin on his face and huge, black pupils. He seems unaware of the tiny, sordid room hung with washing, the sinister men crowding around him watching, and the menacing black cat perched on the stairs above his head. The illustration was apparently inspired by a visit to Bluegate Fields.

Other late 19th century writers were drawn to the East End. In *The Picture of Dorian Gray* (1890) Oscar Wilde writes of "opium dens, where one could buy oblivion, dens of horror where the memory of old sins could be destroyed by the madness of the sins that were new." Arthur Conan Doyle, in 1891's 'The Man With the Twisted Lip', sends Watson on a mercy mission to a Docklands opium den where, inevitably, he discovers Sherlock Holmes in disguise.

A visitor in 1902 summed up the ambience of the opium houses: "There are mysterious looking shops in Limehouse with little or nothing in the windows, and which have curtains to shut off the street. Now and again a Chinaman will push the handle and disappear. It is an opium smoking room. Enter and you will see a counter, a pair of small scales, a few cigars, some tobacco and other etceteras. The shop has a back parlour with a dingy yellow curtain. It is furnished with a settee, chairs, and a spacious divan, or wooden structure with one or two mattresses and half-a-dozen hard pillows or bolsters. It is there that Ya'pian Kan – the prepared opium – is smoked, and the *majoon*, made of hellebore, hemp and opium is chewed, eaten and smoked."[12]

However, the predominant tone from adventurous writers setting out to explore the alien territory of Limehouse Causeway is one of mild disappointment. George Sims, venturing "Off the Track" in 1911, observed only a Chinese boarding house, a grocer's with "a weird Oriental arrangement of shells and seaweed and dried fish" and several young Chinese sailors, one of whom was drinking something that "may be beer." Shops had Chinese names and he did discover an opium den, which was dark and dirty, but no-one wore pigtails or oriental costumes. At the end of Salmon Lane, however, he did find a turtle warehouse which supplied the City and the West End with the key ingredient for "Real Turtle Soup".[13]

Limehouse Nights

The 'yellow peril' panic was not just concerned with a physical threat of 'invasion' in some rather vague form. It was also a moral terror, of white women being corrupted by Chinese men. There were, of course, virtually no Chinese women in Chinatown for most of its existence. In 1881 nine Chinese-born women were recorded in London, and even by 1961 there were fewer than 300 Chinese women in the entire country. This imbalance set the scene for sexual paranoia.

The modern city was still a new, terrifying prospect. Narrow, winding Limehouse streets proved the perfect template for the foreign quarter, a theatre set on which Victorian and Edwardian fascination and revulsion with what they had created was acted out. Thomas Burke was the man who solidified the Limehouse myth in the popular imagination as the dark, dangerous and degenerate Oriental East End. His collection of Chinatown melodramas, *Limehouse Nights*, was published in 1916 and became very popular indeed. In his own words, "It is a tale of love and lovers that they tell in the low-lit Causeway that slinks from West India Dock Road to the dark waste of waters beyond. In Pennyfields, too, you may hear it; and I do not doubt that it is told in far-away Tai-Ping, in Singapore, in Tokio, in Shanghai, and those other gay-lamped haunts of wonder whither the wandering people of Limehouse go and whence they return so casually."[14] It also had a Chinese hero who, despite being referred to as 'The Chink', marks the start of a gradual transition from fear of the Chinese as a mysterious and malign force to some level of acceptance of them as individuals. This process, however, still had some way to go.

Thomas Burke's stories are absurdly melodramatic to modern tastes. They are also distinctly bizarre. Burke was fascinated by corporal punishment, inspired apparently by the schoolgirls of Crouch End, and his books revolve around a disturbing series of personal hang-ups and obsessions, filtered through Limehouse. His books are full of perfect, young, uncorrupted girls abandoned on the streets, where they fall victim to predatory 'Chinamen'. This niche social concern is related to 'weird sex' myths about the Chinese, for example the prevalent belief that they like their women young and doll-like, with bound feet. It is rather more relevant to Burke's own predilections than to anything that was actually happening in Limehouse, but this aspect of his writing seems to have gone unnoticed at the time.

The Insidious Fu Manchu

If Burke was a twisted romanticist, his counterpart was the hard-boiled, adventure writer Sax Rohmer, whose first Fu Manchu novel was published in 1913. Its sensational Chinatown stories about an opium den-dwelling criminal mastermind were exceptionally popular, and stoked the public fascination with the East End to new levels.

Sax Rohmer (a pen name, much more square-jawed than his real one – Arthur Ward), turned a few Limehouse streets into the most notorious neighbourhood in the country during the inter-war years. He was something of a fantasist, claiming to have based Fu Manchu on a real gangster called 'Mr King' who he tracked down for a magazine article, alleged to be "the guiding hand of half the underworld activities of Limehouse".[15] Rohmer's Fu Manchu novels, which he continued writing until 1959, are the ultimate representation of Limehouse Chinatown – a sordid neighbourhood of alleys, tumbledown wharves, and sinister doings in opium dens, naturally. Here 'Chinamen' with fiendish powers lure and imprison white women, until rescued by clean-limbed young Englishmen with the help of the Yard.

The popularity of Fu Manchu encouraged others on to the same territory, including Edgar Wallace who wrote *The Yellow Snake* in 1926, with a Chinese mastermind called Fing Su threatening the West, although he is based rather oddly in Peckham. Agatha Christie took Poirot east in *The Big Four* (1927), with mandatory Chinese mastermind and Limehouse opium den. Another short story, 'The Lost Mine', centres around the Red Dragon club in Limehouse, a respectable gambling establishment with an opium den concealed at the back. The television adaptation of the story features Inspector Japp shaking his head grimly over a recumbent opium smoker and remarking "Passport to paradise, Sergeant".

It has to be said that there is a very good reason why neither Rohmer nor Burke are the household names they once were: their writing is shamelessly racist. There is a direct link between the xenophobic attitudes, Chinese invasion scares, and moral panic of the early 1900s, and the Chinatown of Burke and Rohmer, arch-mythologists of Limehouse. However, Rohmer's books, unlike those of Burke, are still entertaining today and provide a link to a more modern breed of adventure. Fu Manchu is a super-villain of astonishing powers, who can never really be defeated: "Imagine a person, tall, lean, and feline, high-shouldered, with a brow like Shakespeare and a face like Satan… invest him with all the cruel cunning of an entire Eastern race, accumulated in one giant intellect…"[16] In his superpowers and his threat to the very existence of the West he resembles later Bond villains. As the series progressed it moved away from Limehouse, mirroring both the fading myth and the real demise of Chinatown.

The Dope King

At the height of the Chinatown boom, between the 1890s and the 1920s, organised trips took parties of visitors to view the appalling sights of Pennyfields. However, given that the real Chinatown could be a disappointment, the sights were sometimes staged for their benefit. On cue, costumed Chinese men in pigtails would burst from a Limehouse doorway, brandishing cleavers and chasing one another down the street, leaving a satisfied public behind.

The popularity of Chinatown stories went hand-in-hand with the new influence of China across culture in the early 20th century. Chinese exhibitions of costume and design were frequently seen in London, and Chinoiserie was popular in turn-of-the-century music hall. Chinese design and literature were very influential, particularly with modernist artists and writers. Ezra Pound wrote in 1913 that he was "getting orient from all quarters." Pound, Wyndham Lewis, Katherine Mansfield and other writers of their era found an affinity with the reverence of nature and concepts of harmonious balance underlying Chinese culture and literature. They spent time in Chinese-inspired West End bars, particularly the Cave of the Golden Calf in Heddon Street (off Regent Street).

Not everyone was happy about these trends, and some saw Chinatown as a malign influence, corrupting respectable London. H.V. Morton wrote of "Limehouse, that dirty tentacle which the East has

Westferry Arms, Birchfield Street

flung into London."[17] These suspicions were fed by two high-profile, real-life incidents. On 27th November 1918, after attending a Victory Ball at the Albert Hall, Billie Carleton was found dead of an overdose in her Savoy Court flat. She was a singer, just 20 when she died, young, beautiful and rich. The subsequent scandal painted a picture of a 'degenerate' set of bright young things supplied with cocaine and heroin (both recently made illegal) by a Limehouse Chinese man, Lo Ping You and his Scottish wife, Ada. Both were convicted, along with Carleton's contact Reginald De Veulle, and *The Times* led an anti-drugs campaign in response.

In 1922 a similar scandal erupted when a 21-year-old nightclub singer called Freda Kempton, who apparently took cocaine to stay awake while working, died of an overdose in her Westbourne Grove lodgings. She had allegedly been supplied by a Chinese restaurant owner called Billy 'Brilliant' Chang – 'The Dope King' – who the press compared to Fu Manchu. Chang, who had opened London's first Chinese restaurant on Gerrard Street, was acquitted through lack of evidence, but the trial aired a great deal of speculation about his relations with white women and the orgies he supposedly organised.

Broken Blossoms

The Limehouse myth went global when film director D.W. Griffith paid £1000 for the rights to Burke's *Limehouse Nights*. The silent film that resulted, based on the story 'The Chink and the Child', was *Broken Blossoms* (1919). It stars Richard Barthelmess, equipped with full Chinese costume and make-up and a special 'Oriental' posture, protecting wide-eyed innocent Lillian Gish ("Her dreams, her prattle, her bird-like ways") from her brutal father ("A Chink after his kid? He'll learn him") and falling in love with her. Limehouse ("where the Orient squats at the portals of the West") is foggy, ramshackle and tinted blue.

The arrival of Limehouse on screen took Chinatown fantasy to a new level, and it was reported that Thomas Burke thought the film had nothing to do with the reality he claimed to be depicting. He had seeded the myth but now it was far bigger than him, and Hollywood's version of Limehouse was lodged firmly in the collective consciousness. The film's distributors produced advice for cinemas in case anyone thought *Broken Blossoms* libelled the real Limehouse, but it seems that no-one took it too literally.

The film was reflected in the song 'Limehouse Blues', which was made wildly popular by Gertrude Lawrence and covered by everyone from Duke Ellington to Nancy Sinatra. It proclaimed "Oh, Limehouse blues / I've the real Limehouse blues / Can't seem to shake off / Those real China blues / Rings on your fingers / And tears for your crown / That is the story / Of old Chinatown."

Limehouse Blues was also the title of a 1934 docklands crime-and-innocence film with George Raft and Anna May Wong (the first

Chinese-American movie star). She had previously starred in E.A. Dupont's *Piccadilly* (1929), written by Arnold Bennett and a superior offering to most Limehouse films, in which the clubs of the West End lead all too quickly to the opium dens of Limehouse. Its 'Famous dancer found dead in Limehouse' scenario is clearly inspired by the Billie Carleton story. Even Alfred Hitchcock took up the theme in *The Man Who Knew Too Much* (1934), which stages a key scene in a sinister East End Mission Church and features Peter Lorre in his first English language role, every inch the Oriental menace as "Public Enemy No. 1 of all the world".

Although the Chinatown myth was reaching its peak in the years between the wars, in reality a great deal changed when The First World War began. The Hague Convention of 1912, which banned the export of opium, was the first international drug control agreement and spelled the end for the opium dens. Wartime restrictions were introduced on immigration, movements, and opening hours, while most Chinese sailors left to take part in the war effort. The area changed considerably, and was never quite the same place again. Thomas Burke wrote in 1919 that "of colour, mystery and the macabre one must write in the past tense."[18] Much of it he had, of course, invented in the first place.

Death of a neighbourhood

Drug laws may have eliminated the opium dens, but the real changes in Chinatown began with the Aliens Restriction Act of 1919, which made it much more difficult for people from outside the Empire to enter Britain, including the Chinese. The era of an East End dominated by foreign sailors was over, just as the Limehouse myths were reaching their height. The depression of the 1920s had a serious effect on the shipping industry, which proved to be at the start of a long, slow decline.

However, Chinese sailors remained active in Britain, playing a major role in the Second World War. The Chinese Merchant Seamen's Pool of 20,000 sailors was based in Liverpool and manned Atlantic convoys. Many were summarily expelled from Britain after the war was over. The East End Chinese Mission Centre, known as the Flying Angel, still catered to seamen in the late 1960s, and 400 Chinese sailors were still coming into the Port of London every week. But by the end of the 1960s union rules made it difficult for non-British seamen to find work, and many former sailors had moved into the Chinese restaurant business.

The Second World War had a major effect on Limehouse, which suffered extensive bombing. The 'Black Sunday' attacks on the Docks on 7th September 1940 caused serious damage in Chinatown, and many people left straight away. The vast majority of buildings on the streets of Chinatown received some level of bomb damage, as indeed did the whole of Limehouse. Almost every building was marked for clearance, a very different approach to that taken in damaged but prosperous areas of London. Much of this clearance was indeed carried out, leaving little physical trace of the pre-War neighbourhood.

However, as Ian Nairn explains, "Limehouse was done for even before the war, by the wrong kind of rebuilding."[19] The streets around Pennyfields were already in a poor condition in the 1920s, and the London County Council began slum clearance works in the area between Limehouse Causeway and Garford Street in 1932, a process that accelerated after the war. Pennyfields was entirely demolished during the 1950s and 1960s, rebuilt as part of the Birchfield Estate. The Barleymow Brewery, west of Three Colt Street, closed in 1960 and was replaced by the Barleymow Estate. In 1963 a final phase of compulsory purchases removed all traces of the old Chinatown on Limehouse Causeway, Ming Street, Pennyfields and West India Dock Road, and new social housing was constructed. Dan Farson, experimenting with life as an East End pub landlord in the mid-1960s, found a few last traces of Chinatown: a mahjong club called the Chun-Yee on Pennyfields, a Chinese pub, The Commercial, on West India Dock Road, and a restaurant on Mandarin Street called Old Friends with an accompanying photograph of two chefs posing in its doorway, looking distinctly unimpressed.

The two Chinese streets north of the East India Dock Road, Canton Street and Pekin Street, became part of the London County Council's 'Neighbourhood 9' reconstruction area in the late 1940s, and became the site of the highest profile social housing scheme in the country, the Lansbury Estate. Its first phase was designed by architect Frederick Gibberd as a demonstration project, and formed an extension to the 1951 Festival of Britain as the Live Architecture Exhibition. Named after Poplar councillor and Labour leader George Lansbury, the estate consisted of low-rise flats and maisonettes, a market, schools, churches and an impressively strange clock tower on Chrisp Street. Visitors were bussed in to see the new estate, which featured a 200-foot McAlpine's crane, the only one in London; the 'Rosie Lee' Café, a house called 'Gremlin Grange' representing a jerry-built semi from the bad old pre-war days; and the Building Research and Town Planning Pavilions showing the bright way forward. It was not a huge success, being confusing for the casual visitor, and was generally ignored in favour of the main Festival site on the South Bank. However, the complete estate remains intact, likeable if not exactly exciting.

Many Chinese residents who left Limehouse moved to Soho, creating the current Chinatown where the restaurants began to cluster in the early 1960s. The area, seen as disreputable because of its sex shops, was under threat of demolition and rents were cheap. There had also been a small Chinese presence going back to the days of 'Brilliant' Chang. In 1968 there were fewer than 20 Chinese-owned premises; by 1981 more than 50; and now nearly all the businesses in Gerrard Street, Lisle Street, Little Newport Street, Newport Court, Dancey Place, and the relevant sections of Shaftesbury Avenue and Wardour Street are Chinese.

The 2011 census records fewer Limehouse residents of Chinese heritage than in nearby Millwall. Intriguingly though, Chinese businesses have begun, in the last decade, to reappear on Pennyfields. The former Rose and Crown pub is now a Chinese restaurant called 'Noodle St.' and there are signs of other Chinese enterprises nearby. Perhaps Chinatown is quietly rebuilding itself in its former home. If so, will anyone connect the new reality with the old myth, or is Limehouse now so far from the lost mythical neighbourhood that the connection is now broken?

REFERENCES

1   Seton Merriman, Henry, *The Vultures*, The Echo Library 2006

2   Booth, Charles, *Survey Into Life and Labour in London 1886-1903*, LSE Charles Booth Online Archive

3   *ibid*

4   *ibid*

5   *The Times*, 17th July 1900

6   Shiel, M. P. *The Yellow Danger*, Grant Richards 1898

7   Tuchman, Barbara W. *The Proud Tower: A Portrait of the World Before the War 1890-1914*, Hamish Hamilton 1966

8   Witchard, Anne, *Thomas Burke's Dark Chinoiserie*, Ashgate 2009

9   *Daily Express*, 18th June 1919

10   Seed, Dr. John, 'The Chinese in Limehouse 1900-1940', 8th March 2010, untoldlondon.org.uk

11   Anon., 'East London Opium Smokers' *London Society*, July 1868

12   Armfelt, Count E. 'Oriental London' in G.R. Sims (ed.) *Living London: Its Work and Its Play, Its Humour and Its Pathos, Its Sights and Its Scenes*, Vol. 2 Cassell and Company 1902

13   Sims, George R. *Off the Track in London*, Jarrold & Sons 1911

14   Burke, Thomas, *Limehouse Nights: Tales of Chinatown*, Grant Richards 1917

15   Van Ash, Cay and Sax Rohmer, Elizabeth, *Master of Villainy: A Biography of Sax Rohmer*, Tom Stacey 1972

16   Rohmer, Sax, *The Mystery of Dr. Fu-Manchu*, Titan Books 2012

17   *ibid*

18   Witchard, Anne, *Thomas Burke's Dark Chinoiserie*, Ashgate 2009

19   Nairn, Ian, *Nairn's London*, Penguin 1966

OLD ST. PANCRAS: AGAR TOWN, COPENHAGEN AND THE BELLE ISLE

Old St. Pancras persists in fragments, a scattering of pieces left behind by railways, roads and canals.

Introduction

Old St. Pancras persists in fragments, a scattering of pieces left behind by railways, roads and canals. The flamboyant St. Pancras New Church, on Euston Road, is a pretender built when the parish relocated from Old St. Pancras to the more desirable surroundings of Bloomsbury. Its predecessor, St. Pancras Old Church, sits on an obscure mound behind the station, the only solid evidence of the original neighbourhood. The railways ate through everything in their path during 19th century railway fever, including much of Old St. Pancras, replacing the parish with a showpiece station, which is now St. Pancras in the eyes of most people. When its borough was abolished in 1965, Old St. Pancras retreated into the shadows. Buried in its backlands are the remains of a set of little known neighbourhoods that vanished from the map as St. Pancras made the violent transition from hamlet to transport super-hub.

Of these, Agar Town had the shortest, most colourful existence. Before its poorly-built houses were swept away by the Midland Railway it had existed just long enough to become a by-word for the worst of London, a slum everyone had an opinion about and a few had even visited. To the north, Copenhagen was a country estate beyond the edge of London. At first cattle were driven through its fields to slaughter in Smithfield Market, but eventually the slaughterhouses, the cattle trucks and the meat market came to Copenhagen itself. Now they are gone again, as though they had never existed. Belle Isle, nestling in Vale Royal, has hosted London's least pleasant industries for centuries, an out-of-the-way corner with an unlikely mythical double life. These forgotten zones are tucked away out of sight behind the refurbished façades of London's official entrances, at King's Cross and St. Pancras.

Rural and ancient

Myth swirls uncontrollably around the improbable surroundings of King's Cross and St. Pancras, which have been persistently associated with the ancient origins of London. St. Pancras Old Church, with its unusual dedication to a Phrygian boy martyred in 4th century Rome, is said to be one of the oldest in England. A minor industry has developed around its age, including the claim that St. Pancras Old Church is the oldest in the country: "Christ's sacred altar there first Britain saw",[1] asserts an anonymous verse. There is no evidence to support this idea. An altar slab with inscriptions possibly dating from the 7th century was found in the 1840s, although "unsporting scholars"[2] have since dated it to the 1400s. In any case the current church is mostly Victorian but the isolation of this spot, a still centre in the London maelstrom, gives

credence to the idea that it connects with another time.

Dr. William Stukeley, the 18th century antiquary who was not only a clergyman and a Freemason but also a self-taught druid, developed imaginative, widely reproduced theories about St. Pancras. He believed that foundations and ruins in the "the hollow of the hills under Highgate"[3] were the royal palaces of the pre-Roman Kings of Britain, including King Lud and King Lear, descended in a direct line from Brutus, the mythical Trojan prince said to have founded London. This was the Vale Royal, site of Brutus' New Troy or 'Troynovant'.

Stukeley saw a complete, ancient landscape in the Vale Royal. For instance the Brill, a hill to the west of St. Pancras Old Church, was a vast burial mound with underground chambers. He claimed that Julius Caesar's army camped on the Brill, during their British campaign of 54-53 BC. The Brill was real, although now lost under Somers Town where Brill Place marks the spot, but everything else seems to have been summoned into existence by the force of Stukeley's imagination. He was not the only one seeing what he wanted in the landscape. Speculative archaeology reached its peak with the theories about Battle Bridge, the old name for King's Cross which refers to the bridge that once crossed the Fleet. The combination of Romans and 'battle' has led to claims that Boadicea defeated the Romans here, or that she was buried on a site now under one or other of the platforms at King's Cross. This battle did indeed take place somewhere in or around London, but a number of other places lay claim to the battle and to her final resting place.

What we do know about St. Pancras is that there was a small village here in the 13th century with around 40 houses. Ownership of the manor of St. Pancras can be traced back to before 1375. It seems to have been an isolated spot for a long time. John Norden, writing in *Speculum Britanniae* (*The Mirror of Britain*) in the 1590s, says of St. Pancras Old Church, which he describes as being in a bad state of repair, "Yet about this structure have been many buildings,

now decaied, leaving poor Pancrast without companie or comfort."
He adds "Walk not there too late",[4] claiming that it was forsaken by
everyone except thieves.

Springs in the fields

This remained the case until the 19th century. London came to an
end where the British Museum can be found today, and there was
open country all the way to Kentish Town. Tottenham Court Road
trailed away into the fields, leading to a house called Tottenham
Court or Tottenhall Manor at the junction of what are now Euston
and Hampstead Roads. In 1708 the area was rural enough for an
advertisement to read: "At Tottenham Court, near St. Giles's, and
within less than a mile of London, a very good Farm House, with
outhouses and above seventy acres of extraordinary good pastures
and meadows, with all conveniences proper for a cowman, are to be
let, together or in parcels, and there is dung ready to lay on."[5]

Jonathan Swift's *Tale of a Tub*, written in 1704, shows the inhabitants
of St. Pancras Fields as being "innocent of London as if they were
inhabitants of Berkshire" and claimed that they "talk a broad country
dialect".[6] It was, however, no arcadia. Oliver Goldsmith, in a parody
of travel writing from the 1760s, declared: "From Pancrage to Kentish
Town is an easy journey of one mile and a quarter: the road runs
through a fine champaign country, well watered with beautiful drains,
and enameled with flowers of all kinds, which might contribute to
charm every sense were it not that the odiferous gales are often more
impregnated with dust than perfume."[7] The industrial future of Old St.
Pancras was already in evidence.

Apart from the hamlet of St. Pancras, sitting alone beyond Battle
Bridge, there were other reasons for Londoners to venture across
out of town and across Lamb's Conduit Fields. The Adam and Eve
tea gardens were set up on the site of the demolished Tottenham
Court Manor as early as the 1620s and became a popular day trip for

St. Pancras Gardens, Old St. Pancras Church

Londoners, who enjoyed its gardens, good for drinking, smoking and skittles, its speciality cream cakes and a makeshift zoo, which featured "a monkey, a heron, some wild fowl, some parrots, with a small pond for gold-fish."[8] However, the Adam and Eve was not a high class venue, as illustrated by its appearance in an early 19th century poem about a shopkeeper aspiring to be a rake: "Determined to be quite the crack O, / He lounged at the Adam and Eve, / And call'd for his gin and tobacco."[9]

The springs at St. Pancras Wells, next to St. Pancras Old Church, were also a popular 18th century resort. There were extensive gardens beside the River Fleet, which then flowed above ground, and the Wells operated on a grand scale. 'Long rooms' were built to accommodate diners, and entertainment was provided including, apparently, amateur theatre. An advertisement of the 1760s makes it sound rather pleasant:

"St. Pancras Wells Waters are in the greatest perfection, and highly
recommended by the most eminent physicians in the kingdom… the
house and gardens of which are as genteel and rural as any round
this metropolis; the best of tea, coffee, and hot loaves, every day, may
always be depended on, with neat wines, curious punch, Dorchester,
Marlborough, and Ringwood beers; Burton, Yorkshire, and other
fine ales, and cyder; and also cows kept to accommodate ladies and
gentlemen with new milk and cream, and syllabubs in the greatest
perfection."[10] The syllabubs were made by milking cows directly into
glasses of white wine. The popularity of spas and tea gardens had long
gone by the time St. Pancras Wells was demolished in the 1860s for
the new Midland Railway, which drove a swathe through the parish.

Mr. Agar's House

The 19th century saw the land north of the Euston Road transformed
from fields to houses, houses to slums, and slums to railways, wharves,
markets and coal depots in the space of 30 years. It began with the
manor of St. Pancras, which lay between King's Road (now St. Pancras
Way), Maiden Lane (now York Way) and St. Paul's Road (now Agar
Grove). The growth of London led to sudden demand for the manor's
land, and brought sweeping and fundamental change.

A lawyer at the Court of Chancery, William Agar, bought St.
Pancras Manor in 1810 and built his new country retreat, Elm Lodge,
on the site of a house where the notorious Judge Jeffreys had lived
in the 1670s. Agar's new residence was a late Georgian, three-storied
house with a bay at the front. There were mulberry trees in the
grounds, and a long line of poplars linking it to the parish workhouse
nearby, now St. Pancras Hospital.

Agar had chosen a poor location to build a country retreat. Two
years after he moved in, the Regent's Canal Company put forward
plans to build their new canal straight through his land. Agar opposed
them vigorously, and conducted a long-running campaign against

the canal using a combination of legal skills and brute force. His tactics included applying to have company officials committed to the Fleet Prison for contempt of court, and at one stage he even took the company's loss adjuster to court for damaging his crops while assessing their compensation value. He also had his servants barricade the property against surveyors, who nevertheless forced their way in. Bow Street officers were called, and Agar was paid compensation for the intrusion.

In fact, despite his attempts to fight the canal, Agar did very well from the saga. He received £15,750 compensation for the land taken by the canal, a very large sum indeed at the time, and then pragmatically sold the southern part of estate to the Imperial Gas, Light and Coke Company in 1822, as industry arrived in St. Pancras to take advantage of the new canal. The Regent's Canal opened in 1820, running through "Mr Agar's Farm" between Elm Lodge and St. Pancras Workhouse behind what, within 30 years, would be King's Cross Station.

A disgrace

The Regent's Canal was the beginning of a new transport era that would turn a rural parish into an industrial hub. Demolition for the three railway termini that dominate the north side of Euston Road began in the 1830s. The London and Birmingham Railway Company proposed the building of London's first terminus, Euston Station completed in 1837, on land in Somers Town belonging to Lord Somers. He readily agreed, perhaps not realising the destruction that would follow.

Somers Town was, however, no Bloomsbury. The land for both had belonged to Thomas Wriothesely, Earl of Southampton during the late 17th century. He owned the land on which Covent Garden was built, and laid out Bloomsbury Square in 1661, and Bloomsbury passed to the Duke of Bedford through marriage. The Bedford Estate

Reapers Close, Elm Village

became one of the great London estates and was protected from the
railways. The remaining Southampton lands north of Euston Road
were never as fashionable, and Somers Town was not a desirable place
to live.

By the late 18th century London was growing rapidly at its edges,
as the Industrial Revolution began to draw people from the country
to the cities. Most of the buildings on the outskirts were poor quality
and unplanned, a jumble of houses, factories, warehouses, and yards.
New neighbourhoods sprang up that included Pentonville and the
two St. Pancras settlements of Agar Town and Somers Town. Within a
generation meadows outside London had become city slums.

Somers Town outraged John Nash, the architect responsible for
neighbouring Regent's Park. He was unimpressed by the low quality
of the houses springing up next to his fine terraces and said that he

thought Somers Town would "disgrace this apex of the Metropolis".[11] In Somers Town builders created houses that quickly turned into slums, aided by leases that allowed houses to be sub-divided into rooms for let. The not entirely respectable residents of Somers Town were characterised by proto-anarchist William Godwin and his wife, pioneering feminist writer Mary Wollstonecraft, who lived on the Polygon, a curious square with a circle of houses at its centre, later demolished. It was here that Mary died giving birth to her daughter, Mary Shelley. A plaque on Werrington Street marks the spot.

Construction of the railway affected Somers Town badly, and accelerated its descent into poverty. Major work began with the building of Euston Station, which opened in 1838, and continued for much of the 19th century with King's Cross Station opening in 1852, St. Pancras Station in 1868, and the Somers Town Goods Depot and Potato Market in 1887. The latter occupied the large chunk of Somers Town now filled by the British Library and the Francis Crick Institute. Its construction, and that of St. Pancras Station next door, involved the demolition of 15 streets including Brill Crescent, Brill Place and Brill Street, which all disappeared from the map.

A Suburban Connemara

Somers Town became poor very quickly, but Agar Town "was never intended to be anything else"[12], according to historian Gill Tindall. The land on which Agar Town had been built belonged to William Agar. After his death in 1838 the floodgates opened and his country house rapidly disappeared under a sea of jerry building. Agar's widow began to lease out land in 1840, and before long the estate was owned by the Ecclesiastical Commissioners, who managed Church of England land. Agar Town, also referred to as 'Ague Town', had respectable, ecclesiastical sounding streets that gave it the aura on paper of a solid Victorian neighbourhood: Cambridge Crescent, Canterbury Place, Durham Street, Oxford Crescent, Salisbury Crescent, York Place,

Winchester Street. However, its houses were built using poor quality materials and were let on short leases which encouraged exploitative landlords and discouraged maintenance. The Agars let out their land gradually, in small plots, leading to piecemeal development.

The first buildings were Agar Cottages on King's Road (now St. Pancras Way), put up in 1841, and by 1847 Agar Town was nearly complete. It was extended in the mid-1850s on to Agar Fields to the north, but was never larger than a small core of streets straddling the Regent's Canal, squeezed behind the St. Pancras Workhouse. When Agar Town was first built it was said to resemble a shanty town, without paving, drainage or street lighting and "In 1851 – the historical year of civilizing exhibitions – it had gasworks, but no gas"[13] according to the chronicler of ragged London, John Hollingshead.

Agar Town existed at the height of the peculiarly Victorian phenomenon of slum sensationalism. From the mid-19th century, as London underwent a painful transformation into an industrial metropolis, contemporary fascination with the dark side of the city grew and grew, continuing well in the 1900s. The horror of the slums was described and analysed in great detail and, despite the grim realities of poverty in London, with plenty of exaggeration. Slum explorers wrote about expeditions to London neighbourhoods on their doorsteps as though they were visiting uncharted, perilous, foreign territories. There was a tendency to use animal terms such as 'rookery', 'den' and 'colony' to describe alleys, courtyards and dilapidated housing, and to examine the people of the slums as though they were a different species. The frisson of places that were so alien, yet so close at hand, was irresistible to the thrill-seeking reader. It was Agar Town that rose to the top of London's list of shame.

Almost as soon as Agar Town was built, worthies were queuing up to condemn it. John Hollingshead said that it had been "built on a swamp."[14] The Vicar of St. Pancras gave evidence to the House of Lords Committee on Spiritual Destitution, describing Agar Town as a district "of extreme and almost unmitigated poverty. Until the last twelve-month, the main street was unpaved and unlighted and it was scarcely accessible in winter, even to medical men [who would usually pass safely where others would not]. The houses were of the most wretched description, more fitted for the occupation of wild beasts than for human beings."[15]

The archetypal account was 'A Suburban Connemara' by W.M. Thomas, published in Charles Dickens' journal *Household Words*. It told the story of a man moving to London from Manchester who, attracted by the convenience and promising street names of Agar Town, is mostly worried that it will be too expensive for him. When he arrives he finds otherwise: " 'What is the name of this place?' I asked. 'This here, sir?' replied the woman; 'why, Hagar Town.' "[16] In Salisbury Crescent he discovers "...several wretched hovels ranged in a slight curve, that formed some excuse for the name. The doors were blocked up with mud, heaps of ashes, oyster shells, and decayed vegetables." A discussion with a dustman confirmed his poor impressions: " 'It don't much matter in my business, a little dirt, but Hagar Town is worse nor I can abear... The stench of a rainy morning is enough to knock down a bullock.' " Thomas concluded that "In Agar Town we have, within a short walk of the City... a perfect reproduction of one of the worst towns in Ireland."

There was a persistent myth that many of the Agar Town residents had moved from St. Giles, its predecessor as the most notorious and discussed rookery in London which was in the process of being cleared. James King claimed that it had "...such a variety of poor... as to make it a second St. Giles it being very hazardous for any respectable dressed person to pass or repass without insult or annoyance."[17] Thomas Beames wrote that it was "A sample of St. Giles's really in the fields--a collection of the very lowest order of labourers' cottages. There is no occasion to hunt all over the country for samples of overcrowding, dirt, discomfort, and even vice in rural dwellings--here is a Dorsetshire under our very walls, almost within a mile of Temple Bar",[18] which also casts contemporary perceptions of Dorset in an interesting light.

The Real Agar Town

In the face of such opprobrium, Agar Town was doomed from the start and only existed for 20 years before it was eagerly handed over to the Midland Railway Company, to be replaced by the Midland Goods Depot. It was rural in many respects, perhaps an unwelcome reminder of what all cities had been like until the relatively recent past, with chickens, donkeys and knee-high mud in the streets.

It had also became known for knacker's yards, manure heaps, soap manufacture, and other unwanted activities of the kind always banished to the city's poorer areas. Darke's and Starkey's dust yards in particular were "a monster nuisance which impregnate the atmosphere for miles around with the most noxious effluvia arising from the burning of all sorts of filth and refuse."[19] Next to Agar Town were the cinder heaps of Battle Bridge, a "lofty chain of dark mountains"[20], where the dust and refuse such as barley husks from the brewing process were dumped. Charles Dickens was brought up close by, in Baynham Street in Camden and Johnson Street, Somers Town, and this strange landscape is the setting for *Our Mutual Friend*, in which the dust heaps are rumoured to contain gold that will, of course, never be found.

Agar Town certainly suffered from a lack of basic amenities and cheap buildings, but it was not a shanty town. It was alleged that the land was squatted, but in fact the houses were let perfectly legally. There were larger houses in Durham Terrace, the northernmost street, ordinary-sized terraces in Winchester Street, and cottages by the canal in Salisbury Crescent. There were also places where people could build their own houses. One family lived in "a large yellow van upon wheels, thus raised above high mud mark."[21] Beames dismissively described the builder-residents as "always ready to rally round the place, and to call it a 'pretty little town.'"[22] The self-build aspect of Agar Town generated particular condemnation from the *London City Mission Magazine*, which associated Agar Town with "Satan, who has his throne here." Their harsh judgement was based on the belief that most of the houses had been built on "the Lord's Day, when men were industriously building and finishing their dwellings."[23]

Not everyone thought so badly of London's favourite slum. Lord Grosvenor reported that he had seen neat back gardens in Agar Town and thought the people were poor but hard working. However, there was undisguised snobbery at the root of the enthusiastic condemnations. There was a clear division, spatially and socially, between Agar Town and Camden and Kentish Towns to the north, where the houses were larger, better built and much more respectable, and skilled tradesmen had settled. Agar Town's "miserable population of navvies, refuse collectors and casual workers"[24] was of a different social order. *Punch* sneered that it was a place of "awful little by-lanes of two-storied tenements, where patent mangles are to let."[25]

Residents included railway workers employed at the Goods Yard, the depots and the stations nearby. Piano-makers also lived there, as the piano industry was based in Camden with its canal links for transport. There were also costermongers, cat meat dealers and other less than savoury professions. However, more of the inhabitants were labourers, clerks or police constables. There was even a whip maker and a cigar machinist. There was some overcrowding in Agar Town houses, but the one case of a house with six people to a room was exceptional.

Henry Mayhew recorded the street sellers of Agar Town, particularly costermongers and dog and bird-fanciers. Singing birds, caught in the nearby fields, were sold to the locals. Mayhew records a Battle Bridge bird seller called Old Gilham who had been catching 100 birds a week for 60 years. Chickweed and groundsel sellers

St. Pancras Hospital, Granary Street

picked and sold the plants to make tea, and also supplied food for pet skylarks. There were complaints that the noise and smoke from trains was scaring the goldfinches away in Chalk Farm.

Working class heroes Dan Leno and Tom Sayers were both from Agar Town. Leno, king of the music hall, was born there in 1861. Tom Sayers, the boxer, was living in Agar Town when he achieved instant fame in 1860 fighting the American boxer John Heenan, in the first official heavyweight title fight. He beat him despite a broken arm. Sports were played on Agar Fields, and a Mr. Thornley ran a skating rink behind St. Paul's Crescent. Later, those who had lived there as children recalled climbing the walls of 'Counsellor Agar's House' where Miss Agar lived, trying to evade the watchman. They also remembered railway accidents: an engine that fell into Randolph Street from a viaduct, and another that overturned on the embankment behind Wrotham Street.

By 1860 some of the problems that made Agar Town notorious were finally addressed. The Vestry of St. Pancras, responsible for providing services, had refused to do so and accused the Ecclesiastial Commissioners of failing to supply adequate sewers, despite having previously refused to do so themselves. They eventually reached an agreement and the streets were belatedly paved and lit. Ironically, the work was completed just in time for the demolition of Agar Town. The Ecclesiastical Commissioners sold the freehold of the land to the Midland Railway Company.

Demolition

The Midland Railway Company was based in Derby, but its ambitions stretched across the country, and it owned lines as far afield as Belfast and Glasgow. The Midland's extension into London was approved in 1864 despite a great deal of opposition, including from all the rival railway companies, the local vestry, the new Metropolitan Board of Works, the canal companies and the Imperial Gas, Light and Coke Company, all of whom would suffer serious disruption. By this time the company had purchased the land it needed to build St. Pancras Station and its approaches. They first tried to buy St. Pancras Old Church for railway offices, but eventually settled for William Agar's old house, Elm Lodge, instead. The new lines included the Old St. Pancras Tunnel, which was dug 12 feet deep under the graveyard. It was thought this would be deep enough to avoid disturbing bodies, but centuries of use had elevated the ground level so far that they soon found the excavations driving through layers of graves.

The resulting exhumations became a scandal, the Vicar of St. Pancras complaining that trial digging had left skulls and thigh bones strewn around the graveyard. The Home Secretary ordered the works to stop, and appointed a supervisor to make sure bodies were exhumed and removed respectfully. He in turn employed the young

Thomas Hardy, studying to become an architect, to watch over the work. By the time digging finished, in 1867, around 8,000 bodies had been removed and reburied. Hardy wrote a poem, 'The Levelled Churchyard', about the experience which begins "O passenger, pray list and catch / Our sighs and piteous groans, / Half stifled in this jumbled patch / Of wrenched memorial stones!" He is also associated with the Hardy Tree, gravestones symbolically arranged side-on around a tree in the graveyard, although apparently some time after Hardy.

During the first half of 1866 Agar Town and a large area of Somers Town were demolished in the space of two months. The Midland Railway Company put the number of displaced "labouring classes" at 1,180 persons. However, more realistic estimates indicate that 4,000 houses were demolished in Agar, Camden and Somers Towns, displacing perhaps as many as 32,000 people.[26]

A letter to a local paper in 1867 complained that many of the people forced to leave Agar Town had moved north to Gospel Oak, where they were lowering the tone of 'Oak Village', an aspiring development at Lismore Circus (now on the Gospel Oak Estate). An Agar New Town was in fact built just to the north of the original, off Camden Road, but it was not intended for the inhabitants of the original version. New streets – Elm, Lomond and Wrotham Roads – were laid out, and a chunky Byzantine church, St. Thomas the Apostle, was designed by the architect S.S. Teulon. Teulon had been in the process of building a church in Agar Town, which was half completed when the Midland arrived to demolish it. St. Thomas, damaged by bombs and controversially demolished in 1954, was one of two 'compensation churches' that the Midland was obliged to build. The other, St. Luke's on Oseney Crescent in Kentish Town, survives as a replacement for the demolished St. Luke's Euston Road.

The Railway Lands

The site of Agar Town was occupied by the Midland Coal Depot. Coalshoots were built on Camley Street for loading coal onto wagons. Later the Great Northern Railway, operating at King's Cross, constructed its own coalshoots on the opposite canal bank. St. Pancras Canal Basin was dug out in 1867, and used as the Midland coal wharf, unloading coal from barges and taking away ash from locomotives for disposal. York Place and Canterbury Place were bought up separately by the Imperial Gas Company and demolished to build the King's Cross gas holders.

The few remaining streets did not gain from the disruption, becoming blighted by the huge new area of railway sidings, depots, sheds, warehouses and coal heaps. By the 1890s, Cambridge Street was "a wilderness of coal depots".[27] Charles Booth, surveying streets north of the coal depots, claimed that St. Paul's Road "has gone down considerably… only three families in the road keep servants now." On St. Augustine's Road, "The Midland extension has played havoc at the south end" and some of the houses were "not even maintaining the level of shabby genteel."[28]

Maiden Lane (now York Way) gained two stations as what became known as 'the Railway Lands' developed, but both have since vanished. A temporary Great Northern station opened in 1850 to the south of what is now the entrance to the High Speed rail tunnel, as a temporary London terminus for visitors to the Great Exhibition while King's Cross was completed. Also in 1850 a cattle terminal opened at Maiden Lane, on the new North London line, located south of the current Maiden Lane Estate. In 1887 it became a passenger station, but was underused and closed in 1917. Another lost station, King's Cross York Road just to the north of the main King's Cross station, was used by local trains until 1977 when it was demolished. The area also had a tube station, York Road on the Piccadilly Line, which opened in 1906 but was also underused and closed in 1932. The distinctive oxblood tiled station building remains on York Way strangely lacking in transport for an area dominated by rail.

The coal depot and all its workings were demolished in the 1960s when the steam era ended and the Railway Lands entered a long period of dereliction. They formed what was effectively an area of abandoned docks, providing an interchange between rail and canal. A series of long-running planning sagas began. In 1975 the Borough of Camden approved houses on the coal depot site, but construction was put on hold. In 1978 News International considered moving here, before opting for Wapping. Camden then planned to house gypsies here in the 1980s. Part of the Agar Town area became a council tip, and was to become a coach park until Greater London Council created Camley Street Natural Park, which opened in 1984. In the same year Elm Village was built on the rest of the Agar Town site, named after William Agar's Elm Lodge. The streets of Elm Village reflect the isolation of its predecessor, and the area must be one the least visited parts of central London.

Agar Town is commemorated by Agar Grove, a road that existed before it was demolished, then called St. Paul's Road. The only Agar Town street that remains on the map is Granary Street, originally called Oxford Row, which runs behind St. Pancras Hospital. A building from the original Agar Town also remains: the Constitution pub on St. Pancras Way, built by the excellently named Thomas Bolton in 1853.

The Belle Isle

Off York Way, on the southern edge of Copenhagen, the miniature neighbourhood of Belle Isle is a disregarded industrial corner that has always been somewhere to put the most unpleasant industrial activities, a remaining fragment of the dust heaps of Battle Bridge left over when the area was finally developed. In the 19th century Belle Isle contained refuse yards, knacker's yards, chemical manure factories and chemical works. A newspaper from the 1850s complained that "the nuisance makers of Belle Isle are still permitted to affect their neighbours with nausea, sickness, diarrhoea, dysentery and cholera to any extent they please for their own advantage."[29] Charles Booth, visiting in the 1890s, said that Belle Isle "is now and always has been the chief seat of the London horse slaughterers."[30] As well as "many stables" Belle Isle also contained a coal depot, a few cottages, a carpet beating and cleaning factory, and the St. Pancras Iron Works. The streets nearby were home to cabmen, carters, navvies, railway porters and market porters. A local informant claimed that "It stinks like Belle Isle" was a common phrase in the area.

In the 1840s Belle Isle was also home to the Experimental Gardens, known locally as Frenchman's Island. The Frenchman in question was Peter Baume, who lived in London and ran a bookshop and printing press. He was an eccentric who had set up the Society for Promoting Anti-Christian and General Instruction. He came to Belle Isle to form a community run according to the principles of utopian mill owner Robert Owen. Baume let out small plots to allow poor people to build cottages, and attracted a number of radical tradesmen including tailors, shoemakers and their families. By 1851 48 families were living on the site, farming the land co-operatively. George Petrie, a union activist involved with the Experimental Gardens set out their rationale: "The great evil to be regretted… is, that the great bulk of people have been decoyed from the land and agricultural pursuits into cities and large towns, and there are compelled to submit to their masters' terms having no alternative. Let them resolve to return to their lawful inheritance; let them take small allotments of land, and act on the principle we are pursuing."[31]

However, the community attracted hostile attention, and missionaries opened a school to fight the influence of the 'infidel Frenchman'. In 1848 sanitary inspectors found filthy conditions in the Experimental Gardens, which had open drains. Then the new railways begun to intrude. The new Great Northern Line emerged from a

tunnel to the west of the Gardens, while the North London line ran
close by to the south. By 1853 the cottages had mostly disappeared
and the community seems to have been wound up. Belle Isle was
establishing itself as a haven for horse slaughter instead. As early as
1853 a passenger on the NLR complained to the government's Board
of Health of a knacker's yard which not only produced a stench but
subjected rail travellers to the view of parts of dead horses.

Belle Isle remains an industrial pocket in a changing area, home to
factory sheds, offices and the odd nightclub. Its main street sounds
ancient but appears to be recent, having been known as the industrial-
sounding Belle Isle Shoot in the 1860s, probably referring to coal
shoots, before its name was changed to the aspirant Pleasant Lane
and then finally to the mysterious Vale Royal. This ordinary street
with an extraordinary name is the inspiration for the epic poem *Vale
Royal* by Andrew Aidan Dun, which filters the landscape through the
visions of William Stukeley, transfiguring it into the spiritual centre
of occult England. Old St. Pancras Church is placed at the heart of
William Blake's Golden Quatrain, a design for the New Jerusalem in
the 'Valley of Kings'. Dun writes "In wide arcs of wandering the city
/ I saw to either side of what is seen / and noticed treasures where it
was thought there was none."[32] It certainly makes sense that England's
ancient, spiritual heart should be found where few care to look.

In Copenhagen

The growth of London swallowed neighbourhoods further afield than
Agar Town. Immediately to its north lay Copenhagen Fields, and the
name Copenhagen is still occasionally used for an area covering parts
of Barnsbury and the Caledonian Road. Copenhagen Street is the only
other place where the name survives.

Copenhagen Fields were the lands around Copenhagen House,
built around 1620. It may have been constructed to house Danes
during the King of Denmark's visit to his brother-in-law, James I. It

Railway bridge, St. Pancras Way

later became a house of questionable entertainment. By the 1750s there was a tea garden in the grounds, and later in the century it was used for skittles, fives, dog-fighting, bear-baiting, pigeon-shooting, races, boxing, wrestling and cricket. Its licence was revoked in 1816 because of illegal bull baiting and dog fighting.

In 1780 troops were called out by the landlady at Copenhagen House to protect it against the Gordon Rioters, who passed by on their way to burn Lord Mansfield's mansion at Kenwood. By the late 18th century Copenhagen Fields, which were convenient open space on the edge of London, had become a popular venue for demonstrations. In 1795, 40,000 people gathered for a demonstration organised by the London Corresponding Society, which was opposed to war with France.

Most famously, it was the site of the Tolpuddle protest in 1834. A crowd estimated at between 35,000 and 100,000 gathered to protest against the sentences of transportation handed down to the Tolpuddle Martyrs, Dorset agricultural labourers accused of forming an illegal trade union. Led by the Central Committee of the Metropolitan Trade Unions, protestors marched through London to Kennington Common with a wagon carrying a petition with over 200,000 signatures which they attempted, unsuccessfully, to deliver to the Home Secretary, Lord Melbourne. However, the protest worked and the transports were returned from Australia. A contemporary engraving shows the smoking London skyline and the dome of St. Paul's in the distance, and in the foreground a vast crowd filling the fields around Copenhagen House, which sits in open country with the occasional brick-kiln. The march is commemorated by a mural, painted in 1984, on the side of a former pub on Edward Square.

Copenhagen House was still surrounded by countryside and accessible only by footpaths in 1837, but by 1855 London had overtaken it and it had been demolished. However, it had a final lease of life as the Copenhagen House running grounds or 'The Old Cope', which was briefly London's main athletics track. John Garratt opened the track in 1850 in response to legislation which had banned professional running from roads. He introduced the concept of racing for championship belts, and records were set at many distances. In 1852, 16,000 people watched the 10-mile race. The Old Cope closed in 1853 after storm damage, and the land became the Metropolitan Cattle Market.

Buildings had begun to encroach on the Copenhagen Fields in the early 19th century, but nothing was as distinctive or enormous as the new Pentonville Prison. In 1826 Thomas Cubitt bought a substantial section of the fields, probably to make bricks for the construction of Bloomsbury. In 1839 he sold land to the Government for Pentonville

Prison which was designed by Sir Charles Barry as a model prison, with five radiating blocks arranged in a star, intended to keep prisoners separate. It opened in 1842 and became the basic design for prisons across the British Empire, with hundreds built to the same plans in Britain and across the world.

Here Dr. Crippen was executed in 1910, and Irish Republican Roger Casement in 1916. The last person executed here, Edwin Bush, was hanged in 1961. He was the first person convicted using an Identikit and had stabbed a shop assistant to death in a Cecil Court curiosity shop using an antique dagger. Pentonville, which still squats and glowers beside the Caledonian Road is unhelpfully named, being in Copenhagen or Barnsbury if anywhere, but definitely not Pentonville.

I gotta horse!

The slaughter of animals at the ancient Smithfield Market in central London in large numbers had finally become too much by the 1850s and, after public protest over cruelty and nuisance, London's live meat market moved to Copenhagen Fields. The Friday market at Smithfield dated from the 1100s and there was much lamenting when it closed, from drovers in particular: "Mark my words – we may take Sebastopol, but we've lost Smiffield and it's up with the British nation."[33]

The new market opened in 1855 with the main offices, Bank Buildings, on the site of Copenhagen House. It was a huge undertaking, "a monster live-stock emporium"[34] constructed at enormous expense. The centrepiece clock tower still looms over the Caledonian Road, which the original market had four pubs, one at each corner, two hotels, 12 banks and its own telegraph office. Every week 25,000 sheep and 5,000 oxen were sold, not to mention calves and pigs. There were pens for 35,000 sheep and 6,600 bullock-posts. The nearby railways were crucial to the market, with the London and North Western Railway, the Great Northern and the Eastern

Counties bringing 630,000 sheep and 160,000 oxen between them in 1855 alone.

The market was used for the sale and live slaughter of animals, before the meat was transported by lorry to Smithfield. Cows were driven along Market Road on their way to the onsite abattoirs, becoming a strange neighbourhood feature. A typical story, from 1912, tells of an escaped bull which charged into nearby Camden Dwellings and galloped up the stairs to the roof, where it ran around attacking the washing before eventually being shot by a policeman.

From its opening the market site was shared on two days per week by the Pedlar's Market, selling second-hand goods. Despite investment, which included projects such as a Drovers' Hall and Asylum built for aging cattle drovers, trade at the Metropolitan Cattle Market declined gradually and the second-hand market, known as the Caledonian Market, became more prominent.

The glory days for the Caledonian were between the wars when it was the ultimate bric-a-brac market, visited by celebrities including Greta Garbo, Douglas Fairbanks Jnr., Charles Laughton and Gertrude Lawrence. The range of goods was extraordinary. Reports from the 1930s talk about rag stalls, whelk stalls, shrimp stalls, bread and roll stalls, cat and dog meat stalls, tattooists, key cutters, "pistols ancient and modern", a vegetable market, caged birds, rabbits, fowl, ducks, dogs and cats, mice and rats, guinea pigs, monkeys and a bear. A flea circus performed in Greek masks. A man exchanged goldfish and tortoises for brass, old shoes and various types of lumber. In 1932 a woman bought a string of beads at a stall for 7s 6d which, in a national sensation, turned out to be a £20,000 set of black pearls.

Behind the junk market was a section occupied by quacks, fortune-tellers and strong men. A man who sold strength ointment would demonstrate its effects by bending iron bars and hammering nails into wood with his bare hands. The market also specialised in quick-fire salesmen, known by the market men as 'fannies', whose patter mesmerised customers into buying patent cleaning polishes and the like. The Caledonian Market's most famous character was Prince Monolulu, an Ethiopian tipster who dressed in red and purple robes and a crown and would shout "I gotta horse! I gotta horse!"

The Caledonian Market reached the end in 1939 when it was requisitioned by the Army as a storage depot for vehicles, becoming a Royal Mail van depot after the war. Despite a petition signed by 13,500 people, the market was moved to Bermondsey, where it still trades as the New Caledonian Market, specialising in antiques.

The Cattle Market and its slaughterhouses remained in use for much longer. Until 1953 cows were herded along Market Road, from railway sidings in Piper Close opposite Caledonian Road tube station, to slaughter at the market. Eventually the site was closed in 1963 and the Market Estate built on the site in 1967. It then spent nearly 40 years deteriorating, and was partly demolished and replaced in 2005.

Signs of the market are unmistakable, despite the waves of change. Apart from the distinctive clock tower, the tallest building in the area, three of the four corner pubs survive – the Lamb, the Lion, and the White Horse – although none are open as pubs any more. The fourth, the Black Bull Hotel, was converted into a wicker factory after it closed following the murder of one of its barmaids. It then burned down in the 1930s. Caledonian Park is on part of the market site, and the remainder is occupied by the Market Estate, rebuilt in the 2010s after decades of neglect and notoriety.

St. Pancras is still a fiendishly complicated maze of apparently unrelated places, separated by the sprawling railway structures that split the neighbourhood apart within the space of two mid-19th century decades. Building on the Railway Lands behind King's Cross, the largest development site in London, is finally underway after 40 years of argument. However, the new offices and flats belong to a new version of King's Cross rather than Old St. Pancras. While new buildings have changed the previously seedy streets around King's Cross Station, places such as Elm Village, the Maiden Lane Estate, Belle Isle and the Copenhagen end of the Caledonian Road are as much off the radar as they ever were. They have always been off the radar, places apart, near at hand yet bypassed by all, and nothing has changed.

REFERENCES

1   Anon. quoted in Walford, Edward, *Old and New London: Volume 5*, Cassell 1878

2   Bradley, Simon, *St. Pancras Station*, Profile Books (2007)

3   Dun, Aidan Andrew, *Vale Royal*, Dark Star (2010)

4   Norden, John, *Speculum Britanniae* quoted in Walford, Edward, *Old and New London: Volume 5*, Cassell 1878 (1593)

5   The *Postman*, December 30th, 1708

6   Swift, Jonathan (1996, originally published 1704) *A Tale of a Tub and other works*, Oxford: Oxford University Press

7   Goldsmith, Oliver, *The Citizen of the World*, R. Morison and Son Ltd. (1762)

8   Walford, Edward, *Old and New London: Volume 5*, Cassell 1878

9   Smith, James and Smith, Horace, *Rejected Addresses or the New Theatrum Poetarum*, John Miller (1812)

10   Walford, Edward, *Old and New London: Volume 5*, Cassell 1878

11   Porter, Roy, *London: A Social History*, Penguin (1994)

12   Tindall, Gillian, *The Fields Beneath*, Temple Smith (1977)

13   Hollingshead, John, *Ragged London in 1861*, Smith, Elder and Co. 1861

14   *ibid*

15   Denford, Steven L.J. *Agar Town: The life and death of a Victorian "slum"*, Camden History Society 1995

16   Thomas, W.M. 'A Suburban Connemara', *Household Words*, 8th March 1851

17   J.F. King quoted in Lovell, Percy and Marcham, William McB., *Survey of London: Volume 19*, London County Council (1938)

18   Hollingshead, John, *Ragged London in 1861*, Smith, Elder and Co. 1861

19   *The Builder*, 14 Oct 1854

20   Thomas, W.M. 'A Suburban Connemara', *Household Words*, 8 March 1851

21   *ibid*

22   Hollingshead, John, *Ragged London in 1861*, Smith, Elder and Co. 1861

23   *London City Mission Magazine*, 1846

24   Inwood, S., *A History of London*, Macmillan (1998)

25   *Punch*, 1845

26   Dyos, H.J., "Railways and Housing in Victorian London" *Journal of Transport History*, Vol. 2, No.1 (May 1955)

27   Booth, Charles, *Survey Into Life and Labour in London 1886-1903*, LSE Charles Booth Online Archive

28   *ibid*

29   *Metropolitan*, 13 Sept 1856

30   Booth, Charles, *Survey Into Life and Labour in London 1886-1903*, LSE Charles Booth Online Archive

31   Coates, Chris, *Utopia Britannica*, Diggers and Dreamers 2001

32   Dun, Aidan Andrew, *Vale Royal*, Dark Star 2010

33   Edwards, Marjorie, *Up the Cally: the history and recollections of London's Old Caledonian Market*, Marketprompt 1989

34   Hollingshead, John, *Ragged London in 1861*, Smith, Elder and Co. 1861

CHURCH HILL

THE OLD ROSE

RATCLIFF: SAILOR TOWN

The name 'Ratcliff' has faded into almost complete disuse, but for 350 years it linked the thriving mercantile capital to imperial ports and global trade routes around the world.

Introduction

The name Ratcliff* derives from the Red Cliff, a bank of light-red gravel which once rose from the Thames above Wapping Marsh. The gravel is now impossible to detect, much of it dug out and distributed around the globe as ballast in the ships that left Ratcliff for destinations far and wide. Ratcliff, the place that grew up by the river, is also depleted and hard to locate after a century of change and decline. It was once the beating heart of London's river trade, but suffered with the decline and fall of maritime London. The name 'Ratcliff' has faded into almost complete disuse, but for 350 years it linked the thriving

---

* The spelling of Ratcliff has constantly shifted, equally often spelled Ratcliffe, Radcliff or Radcliffe. John Stow's 1598 *Survey of London* used three different versions on a single page; and the issues was still unresolved in the early 1900s, when the London County Council tried to revive 'Ratcliffe' as the supposedly authentic, olde worlde spelling. This chapter uses 'Ratcliff', which seems to be the currently favoured version, but other forms also find their way into the text depending on context.

mercantile capital to imperial ports and global trade routes around the world.

Once known as 'Sailor Town', Ratcliff was a hamlet when shipbuilders, ship-owners, captains, merchants and crew began to arrive during the reign of Elizabeth I. They built wharves to anchor vessels at what was the closest practical landing spot for large vessels to the City of London. The rapid growth of East London during the 19th century began with the Docks and, as the City expanded, it enveloped Ratcliff which found itself the underbelly of a vast new industrial capital. Ratcliff gained a different reputation, as a place that represented the very worst of London. It offered a thousand morality tales in one neighbourhood, just a cab ride from Fleet Street.

One hundred and fifty years on Ratcliff has been systematically dismantled, broken up by a combination of post-war deconstruction and post-industrial reconstruction. Both its previous fame and its notoriety may have faded, but enough remains to hint at a vivid, lost London hovering just beyond our reach.

A place of shifting identity

Ratcliff is one of the nine 'tower hamlets'[1] originally owned by the Tower of London. By the early 17th century it was the largest, and London's shipping centre. The name Ratcliff still appears on maps, squeezed between Shadwell, Limehouse and The Highway, which quarantines the former dock neighbourhoods behind lanes of heavy goods vehicles. However, within the modern London Borough of Tower Hamlets Ratcliff no longer exists even as a council ward. This is the end point of a 500-year ride from wealth and fame to notoriety, and finally almost complete obscurity.

Sensitivity over Ratcliff's status goes back a long way. Starting as a hamlet in the parish of Stepney, it eventually became large enough to break free and become a parish in its own right in the 19th century. Until then "the precedence of the Ratcliff churchwarden was jealously maintained" at Stepney's church, St. Dunstan's, "for it was held that of all the hamlets lying within the ancient parish of Stepney, the antiquity of Ratcliff gave to it the premier place"[2] according to 1930s local historian Sydney Maddox. The links between the Docks and the church are also strong: St. Dunstan's is known as 'the Church of the High Seas' and its graveyard contains monuments to admirals, rear-admirals, captains and ship-owners.

After its status as a port had faded Ratcliff was eventually subsumed into Tower Hamlets, but it had already been encroached upon by the districts of Limehouse and Wapping. Neighbouring Shadwell, with a tube station to back up its claims, has now become the accepted name for much of the area that was formally Ratcliff.

From hamlet to port

We know that the stretch of Thames at Le Redeclyve, as it was known, was used by ships in the Middle Ages. The first wharf is recorded here in 1348. Ships from Edward III's navy were built, fitted out and provisioned here in the 1370s for the unsuccessful wars with France led by John of Gaunt. Geoffrey Chaucer worked in Ratcliff for seven years during this time from 1374, as Controller of the Customs and Subsidies of Wools, Skins and Hides for the Port of London.

Ratcliff grew in size and fortune along with London's port, which was becoming established during the reign of Elizabeth I. Up until then it was a handful of houses, separated from the City of London by Wapping Marsh. When the marsh was drained at the end of the 16th century, houses were built along the Thames linking Ratcliff to the City. Writing in 1598, John Stow complained about the speed of change east of the Tower of London: "From this precinct of St. Katherine to Wapping in the west… was never a house standing within these forty years." However, "there hath been of late, in place of elm trees, many small tenements raised towards Radcliffe".[3]

Stow blamed this East London housing boom on the removal

of the gallows, which he suggested had previously put people off living there. Along the shoreline at Wapping, the bodies of executed "pirates and sea rovers" were left hanging long after execution. His notes record that "since the gallows being after removed further off, a continual street, or filthy strait passage, with alleys of small tenements, or cottages, built, inhabited by sailor's victuallers, along by the river of Thames, almost to Radcliff, a good mile to the river."[4]

The spread of naval shipbuilding from the Royal Dockyard at Deptford to Ratcliff, as well as to Blackwall further downstream, triggered 150 years of population growth. The Stepney Vestry Minutes of 1641 record that "whereas the Hamlet of Ratcliffe is of late so largely increased, by the multitude of the same is found to be a burden too heavy for one church warden." The growth of the new East End, later to become the engine room for a global Empire, began in Ratcliff.

At Ratcliff Cross

'Sailor Town' had its origins at Ratcliff Cross, a landing place on the Thames at the western end of what is now Narrow Street. The Cross itself was removed some time after 1732, but the stone slipway to the Thames foreshore at Ratcliff Cross Stairs still marks the location of the quay. Not far away Ratcliffe Cross Street, a now dilapidated lane between Cable Street and Commercial Road, was the site of the Ratcliff Market.

The Ratcliff Cross itself carried a ceremonial significance that has now faded from memory. Walter Besant wrote in 1901 that Victoria had been acclaimed as Queen at Ratcliff Cross among other London locations, but by 1901 the reasons had already been forgotten.[5] The status of the cross presumably reflected the significance of London's first port, and was a thing of the past by the 20th century.

Ratcliff Cross was more notable as a place where boats could be hired to cross the Thames. Samuel Pepys, like other Londoners of his time, travelled so frequently by water that his Diaries specify journeys

Chigwell Hill, off Ratcliffe Highway

that were made 'by land'. He would often walk to Ratcliff from his house near the Tower, and take a boat to the naval dockyards at Deptford where he had business. The East End still has no Thames bridge of its own, with the river crossings here built as tunnels to maintain access for shipping to the Pool of London Docks. This gives Ratcliff and this stretch of riverside a continued air of separation from the south bank of the river.

Samuel Pepys also visited Ratcliff to commission naval charts for Charles II and senior officials, from a 'platemaker' based on Ratcliff Highway. Naval industries clustered in the newly expanding hamlet as the 17th century progressed. Other industries gathered here too: Ratcliff Crown glass was manufactured from the late 1600s in a factory on Broad Street and was famous as Britain's first plate window glass, each pane embossed with a crown symbol.

Ratcliff was at the centre of Tudor England's growing dominance of the seas. Early explorers departed on voyages from Ratcliff Cross Stairs, not always making it back. In 1553 Sir Hugh Willoughby sailed the Bona Aventura and two other ships to the seas north of Russia, looking for a north-east passage to Cathay. Sir Hugh died, along with the crew of two of his ships, off the coast of North Norway, but the third captain, Richard Chancellor, reached Archangel and opened a new trade route to Moscow.

Sir Martin Frobisher sailed from Ratcliff on three expeditions in the 1570s, reaching Greenland and Canada and 'discovering' the mythical Atlantic island of Buss. When subsequent explorers failed to confirm the existence of Buss, it was reported as having sunk. In Greenland Frobisher discovered a type of black rock that he believed contained gold which, after a major expedition to bring tons of it back to England, turned out to be worthless. It was instead used for building, and a black stone wall in Dartford survives today, made from Frobisher's fool's gold. A ceramic plaque, located in King Edward Memorial Park by the ventilation shaft for the Rotherhithe Tunnel, commemorates the Elizabethan adventurers with a charming 1920s illustration of ships under full sail.

Other mariners, less famous but equally influential, were based in Ratcliff. John Vassall, who lived on Broad Street, was one of the founders of Virginia. In 1588 he fitted out two ships and sailed from Ratcliff to join the fight against the Spanish Armada. Thomas Best opened the routes to India when he defeated the Portuguese at sea in 1611 and 1612. Senior figures in the founding of the East India Company and of Trinity House (responsible for lighthouses) also lived near Ratcliff Cross.

Ratcliff burns

Ratcliff was included in the new parish of St. George-in-the-East in 1729, by which time it had become a populous neighbourhood.

However, the warehouses and the tenements of which John Stow had disapproved were swept away in the Ratcliff Fire of July 1794. Fires were not unknown among the largely wooden houses and warehouses but this one was unusually disastrous, one of the largest fires that burned in London between The Great Fire and the Blitz. It began on the waterfront, at the East India Company's Free Trade Wharf, which was used to store volatile saltpetre, an ingredient of gunpowder. When it caught light the resulting explosion and fire destroyed 458 homes and 20 warehouses in the course of a few hours. The fire engulfed most of Ratcliff and a dramatic engraving from the time, 'The Ruins of Ratcliffe', shows ships at anchor off a wrecked riverfront, eerily similar to the later images of Second World War bomb damage.

The oldest surviving buildings in Ratcliff, apart from St. George-in-the-East Church, were built after the fire which cleared the way for more substantial, brick houses. A row of Queen Anne terraced houses survives on Narrow Street, including the well-known Grapes pub, as does the Master's House on Butcher Row. This became the vicarage for Ratcliff's own church, St. James', which was destroyed by bombs when Ratcliff burned again in 1940. Free Trade Wharf was rebuilt after the fire, and still stands on the Thames near Jardine Road with the East India Company's coat of arms over its gates. Typically for the modern, patchwork version of Ratcliff it is dwarfed by a 1980s apartment complex also called Free Trade Wharf, which looms next door like an outsized, red brick anthill.

Maps from 1799 show Ratcliff, facing towards the river and away from the rest of London, still separated from Stepney by fields to the north. Both Ratcliff and neighbouring Limehouse were dominated by timber yards and by rope walks: long, narrow rope-making workshops which reflected the shape of their product. Some were astonishingly long, with those on Ratcliff Fields (later called Sun Tavern Fields and now covered by the Glamis Estate) a quarter of a mile from end to end. Their size is placed in context by the large sailing vessels they

Ropemaker's Fields, Limehouse

supplied, which were equipped with as many as 20 miles of rope. The ropewalks were particularly unpleasant and dangerous places to work, featuring both hot tar and hemp dust, which was volatile and liable to explode. Commercial Docks and wharves lined the river with Free Trade Wharf, rebuilt after the fire and worryingly still used to store saltpetre. Nearly all the businesses existed to serve ships: ship chandlers, mast-makers, sail-makers, anchor-smiths, coopers, butchers and ship's biscuit bakers, as well as a brewery and a large distillery.

Until the first enclosed docks opened, ships anchored in the Thames and off-loaded at wharves. The new London Docks, carved out of the Isle of Dogs, changed all that. Opening in the 1790s they took 15 years to complete and were London's first basins, sited between Ratcliff and the City. Five docks were built: the large Western and Eastern Docks, and the smaller Tobacco Dock, Hermitage Dock and Wapping (later

Shadwell) Basin. This amounted to 2½ miles of quays and jetties with room for hundreds of ships, all enclosed behind a high dock wall to keep valuable goods safe.

The new London Docks were used by short sea traders: small ships designed for trips from the Continent. They delivered food – tinned and dried – spices, tobacco, wool and ivory. The new docks began to shift the focus from the traditional centre for shipping at Ratcliff towards Wapping which, along with places further afield, now had the facilities to handle much larger volumes of merchant shipping. Although Ratcliff would remain 'Sailor Town' for another century it had relied on its wharves, and the evolution of the Port of London meant the end was already in sight for its time as the senior hamlet. However, it did not go quietly.

As the port grew, workers were drawn to Ratcliff and the surrounding dock neighbourhoods. The population of Ratcliff grew from 5,000 in 1801 to 17,000 by 1861, by which time the hamlet had been absorbed into a much expanded area of docklands that covered both sides of the river. Many Irish people in particular arrived to work the Docks, with an estimated 14,000 living in Ratcliff and Shadwell by the early 1800s. Conditions deteriorated as housing became increasingly overcrowded while the employment offered by the port was casual and precarious, particularly in the era of sail when adverse winds or ice could prevent ships from docking.

Casual labour was often supplied by the owners of local taverns, who controlled both accommodation and jobs, but the men they employed to work the wharves complained that they were not always paid, or were fobbed off with second-rate goods instead of wages. During the late 18th century this occasionally led to serious trouble, including a riot in Stepney Fields involving sailors and coal-heavers which led to fatalities, and the hanging of seven coal-heavers on Sun Tavern Fields convicted of shooting at the landlord of the Roundabout Tavern in Shadwell. Earlier the landlord, John Green, had been acquitted although he was uninjured and had shot two protestors dead outside his tavern. The road adjacent to the Fields was called Cutthroat Lane (now Brodlove Lane) during this era which hints at the less-than-genteel character of the area.

A cursed place

Despite its illustrious naval and merchant history, if Ratcliff is remembered at all today it is for two grim days in December 1811. Late on Saturday 7th December a man called Timothy Marr, owner of a draper's shop at 29 Ratcliff Highway, sent his maid Margaret out for oysters. When she returned (without the oysters) the door was locked and there was no answer. Eventually, carnage was discovered inside: Marr lay dead behind the counter; his wife Celia stretched out nearby; their apprentice, James Gowen, at the back of the shop; and their three-month old baby Timothy in his cradle. All their throats were cut and their skulls had been crushed with a shipwright's maul (a hammer with a long handle and pointed head).

Violence, again apparently without motive, erupted again 12 days later. Passers-by witnessed a terrified man using knotted sheets to climb from an upstairs window at the King's Arms pub on New Gravel Lane (now Garnet Street). He was a lodger, fleeing from the slaughter taking place inside. The pub's landlord, John Williamson, his wife Elizabeth and their maid Anna Harrington had all been murdered, in the same gruesome manner as the Marrs. Meanwhile their granddaughter, Kitty, had slept through it all on the top floor.

The fury and panic over these inexplicable killings found a focus two weeks later when the rudimentary police force of the time arrested, together with several others, a sailor called John Williams who was lodging at the Pear Tree pub on Cinnamon Street, off Ratcliff Highway. Four days later he hanged himself in his cell at Coldbath Fields Prison, leaving unresolved doubts over whether he was the real murderer. Cheated of an execution, the authorities instead chose to parade his body on a cart through Ratcliff, past the houses of his supposed victims. At the junction of Cable Street and Cannon Street Road, for reasons that remain unclear, they drove a stake through his heart before burying his body at the crossroads, the traditional grave of a suicide.

Public fear and outrage triggered an East End panic that prefigured the horrified fascination with Jack the Ripper, 77 years later. Thomas de Quincey wrote an infamous satirical essay, 'On Murder Considered as One of the Fine Arts', in which he declares the killings "The most superb of the century by many degrees" and says of John Williams "All other murders look pale by the deep crimson of his."[6]

This grisly sequence of events cemented Ratcliff's reputation as a lawless, dangerous place and also began the process of erasing it from the map. Ratcliff Highway became such a loaded street name that it was quietly abandoned, and the road divided into new stretches with different names. Part of it became St. George's Street, which even in the 1930s was described in a London guidebook as "a modern name which hardly disguises the former notorious Ratcliff Highway".[7] It is now called The Highway, a name which, in partially concealing its past, only seems to amplify the echoes.

John Williams' skeleton was rediscovered in 1886 by workmen digging a gas main, and seems to have been divided up into souvenirs. His skull allegedly ended up behind the bar at the Crown and Dolphin pub (still standing but now divided into flats, the final tenant having died in 2010) at the crossroads where he was buried. The location, of no apparent significance on the ground, has acquired mythical status because of the burial and plays a central role in occult re-readings of the East End.

However, most of the other locations associated with the murders have gone from the map, reflecting the gradual dismantling of Ratcliff. The King's Arms was demolished in the 1830s for an extension of the London Dock, which chewed a large, watery hole in the centre of the

Oyster shells, riverside, Ratcliffe stairs

district. Timothy Marr's shop, near Artichoke Hill, was still standing in 1928 and "very markedly the ramshackle place fits the frightful scenes of which it was the setting."[8] It vanished, along with the Pear Tree pub and much of the surrounding area, during the Blitz, which visited particular destruction on Ratcliff. Peter Ackroyd, who fictionalised the murders in his novel *Dan Leno and the Limehouse Golem*, felt the need to relocate his version to Limehouse, probably a more marketable location.

The horrors of the Highway

During the 19th century Radcliff built a new reputation as the home of everything that Victorian London loved to hate. There was no shortage of writers, particularly during the 1850s and 1860s, who could barely contain their glee at the exotic excitements so conveniently close to home, Thomas de Quincey reflected the feverish fascination that was buzzing around 'Sailor Town' by the 1850s. In a postscript to 'On Murder' he described the "manifold ruffianism shrouded impenetrably under the mixed hats and turbans of men whose past was untraceable to any European eye."[9] In *The Wild Tribes of London*, which gives it all away in the title, Watts Phillips writes: "Ratcliffe-highway by night! The head-quarters of unbridled vice and drunken violence-of all that is dirty, disorderly, and debased. Splash, dash, down comes the rain; but it must fall a deluge indeed to wash away even a portion of the filth to be found in this detestable place."[10]

The unexpected *Taxi Driver* resonances are typical of the moral verdicts passed on Ratcliff. Anthropologist J. Ewing Ritchie analyses the Highway in ominous style: "I should not like a son of mine to be born and bred in Ratcliffe-highway." He adds obscurely that "In beastliness I think it surpasses Cologne with its seven and thirty stenches, or even Bristol or a Welsh town." He blames hard drinking sailors or 'crimps' for the drunkenness, dancing and fighting he claims to have witnessed.

The local press joined in the fun, with a particularly condescending piece on the "interesting young ladies" who frequented the Ratcliff Highway: "Twenty of them to disguise themselves in masquerade dresses, and cram themselves into and on several cabs and then in solemn procession parade up and down the Highway, halting occasionally at some hostelry to drink fiery blue sulphuric acid sold under the name of gin. Then they start again. See the first cab: inside tawdry spangles, broke feathers, soiled muslins, gin bleared eyes, and shrunken arms wildly gesticulating from the windows."[11] This particular article then descends into a list of spluttering imprecations: "Drunkenness and noise–vice and blasphemy–robbery and obscenity by day–flaring gas lights–blue sulphuric acid–drunkenness and noise–vice and blasphemy–robbery and obscenity by night; and added to these–blood–murder."[12]

Ratcliff also drew attention for the presence of foreign sailors, who were every bit the exotic mix: "Up and down Ratcliffe-highway do the sailors of every country under heaven stroll – Greeks and Scythians… Lascars, Chinese, bold Britons, swarthy Italians, sharp Yankees, fair-haired Saxons, and adventurous Danes – men who worship a hundred gods, and men who worship none",[13] wrote proto-tabloid journalist J. Ewing Ritchie.

Foreigners took the blame for much of the mayhem. An account in the *East London Observer* claimed "Either a gin-mad Malay runs a much [sic] with glittering kreese [a Malay dagger], and the innocent and respectable wayfarer is in as much danger as the brawler and the drunkard; or the Lascar, or the Chinese, or the Italian flash their sea knives in the air, or the American 'bowies' a man, or gouges him, or jumps on him, or indulges in some other of those innocent amusements in which his countrymen delight."[14]

The Prospect of Whitby pub on Wapping Wall (named after a collier, a ship that carried coal from the Tyne) is a famous relic of the 19th century riverside. There has been a pub here since the early 1500s, but the Prospect became famous when Charles Dickens disguised it thinly as The Six Jolly Fellowship Porters and set much of *Our Mutual Friend* in its bar. The pub is "of a dropsical appearance" with "not a straight floor, and hardly a straight line."[15] It serves reviving Victorian drinks such as "burnt sherry", "mellow flip" and hot brandy and water.

At the centre of everything in Ratcliff is the promise of the river and the reality of the mud. In *Our Mutual Friend* the "harbour of everlasting mud"[16] oozes into the streets. Turn-of-the-century accounts describe children who "would stand on Ratcliffe Cross Stairs and gaze out upon the rushing tide and upon the ships that passed up and down. At low tide they ran out upon the mud, with bare feet, and picked up apronfuls of coal to bring home. Needs must that a child who lives within sight of ships should imagine strange things and get a sense of distance and mystery".[17] Dickens' Ratcliff is "a place of poverty and desperation, where accumulated scum of humanity seemed to be washed from higher grounds, like so much moral sewage, and to be pausing until its own weight forced it over the bank and sunk it in the river."[18] It is depicted as isolated and semi-derelict, with boatmen inhabiting disused mills beside the river and making a living fishing dead bodies from the Thames.

But Ratcliff's notoriety was relatively short-lived. The press coverage had an effect, and the police took a firmer grip of the neighbourhood. By 1879, what "until within the last few years was one of the sights of the metropolis, and almost unique in Europe as a scene of coarse riot and debauchery, is now chiefly noteworthy as an example of what may be done by effective police supervision",[19] according to Charles Dickens' Jnr.'s *Dictionary of London*. On Shadwell High Street an Irish pub, the White Swan, or 'Paddy's Goose', was "once the uproarious rendezvous of half the tramps and thieves of London, now quiet, sedate, and, to confess the truth, dull–very dull."[20] By the 1890s, Charles Booth was describing the areas as "formerly the notorious Ratcliff Highway but its palmy days are over." However, he noted that the shops were "still redolent of the sea".[21]

From docks to decay

The London Docks remained the main transit point for goods and exotic produce from across the globe. Broad Street, now The Highway, was so close to the action that you would see ships' bowsprits "projecting across the road and almost touching the window of the house opposite the dry dock." The street was "redolent of odours strange and varied – hay, ship's biscuits, coals, tarred twine, horses, brewers' grains, paint, kippers, coffee, stale beer, and the mustiness of water-logged wood."[22]

Louis-Ferdinand Céline applied his unique style to evoke a violent, queasily unstable version of the London Docks during the 1910s: "…the warehouses, all-brick giant ramparts… Treasure cliffs!… monster shops   phantasmagoric storehouses, citadels of merchandise, mountains of tanned goatskins enough to stink all the way to Kamchatka!… Enough sponges to dry up the Thames! What quantities!… Enough wool to smother Europe beneath heaps of cuddly warmth… Himalayas of powdered sugar… Matches to fry the poles!… Enormous avalanches of pepper, enough to make the Seven Floods sneeze!… A thousand boatloads of onions, enough to cry through five hundred wars… Coffee for the whole planet!…"[23] While Céline's specifics could perhaps be questioned, there is no doubt he captures the exoticism of the London Docks at their peak.

Charles Booth, visiting Ratcliff in 1895, found a mixed area including poverty and dereliction, and houses in poor condition or partially demolished. While next door Stepney was middle-class, Ratcliff was a step down the ladder. At the centre, around Butcher Row, he described "loose women, 'sailor's widows'" and "rough loafers". The worst streets were semi-demolished, with broken windows stuffed with rags. The better streets were clean and children were "booted, but ragged".[24] Céline also describes Ratcliff itself in decay: "Two more blind alleys, a completely deserted market… and then the rubble of a fire… and then a tiny square, a lamppost right in the middle, three putrid houses, ought to be torn right down…"[25]

This is precisely what happened during the Blitz, which destroyed many buildings in Ratcliff as the Luftwaffe targeted the Docks. However, Ratcliff's last moment in the spotlight came just before the bombs. On 4th October 1936, 100,000 anti-fascist marchers gathered on Cable Street, its main east-west road, and successfully prevented Oswald Mosley's anti-Semitic British Union of Fascists from marching through the Jewish East End. A mural on the side of the former Stepney Town Hall commemorates the Battle of Cable Street. It has been vandalised several times, and artists who have worked on it have suffered intimidation from the far-right, suggesting the battle is not yet over.

Cable Street pediment

Cable Street today is an underwhelming, emasculated thoroughfare but the Victorian Thames House complex, at the heart of Ratcliff on the junction with Butcher Row, provides evidence of pre-war Ratcliff. It was one half of the Batger's Confectionery Factory, responsible for products such as Chinese Figs, Good News Crackers, and Silmo's Lollies, familiar from evocative 1920s adverts. The other half of the factory, across the road, was destroyed and the firm moved out leaving an empty complex behind as a monument to Ratcliff's lost industry.

The war-time destruction led to major redevelopment, resulting in new-build council estates and roads on a scale unsuited to a residential area. However, although Ratcliff was no longer commercially significant, and had become physically fragmented, its reputation lingered past the Second World War. Ian Nairn, writing in 1966, found something to admire in a familiar image of Ratcliff: " 'Cable Street, the whore's retreat': a shameful blot on the moral landscape of London: an outworn slum area… all that is left of lurid Dockland. Its crime is not that it contains vice but that it is unashamed and exuberant about it."[26]

This is no longer the case, at least not in public, and exuberance is not a word associated with Ratcliff. The street patterns remain recognisable from 1811 but planning interventions, as well as bombing, unpicked the physical coherence of the area. Large-scale demolition was required for the building in the 1890s of the Rotherhithe Tunnel, which surfaces in what had previously been the centre of Ratcliff. Large, busy roads are now one of its defining characteristics, with the Highway and the Limehouse Link tunnel (for many years the most expensive road in Britain) cutting across the neighbourhood.

Next to the tunnel entrance, on the site of the bombed St. James' Church, is a curious neighbourhood in exile. The Royal Foundation of St. Katharine is a Royal Peculiar reporting directly to the monarch, separate from its surrounding diocese. It is an island within Ratcliff that officially belongs elsewhere. The Foundation was forced to relocate from its original site next to the Tower of London when its neighbourhood was demolished for the controversial building of St. Katharine's Dock in 1827 and it eventually settled permanently in Ratcliff in 1948, taking over the rebuilt St. James'.

The riverfront enjoys a separate existence from inshore Ratcliff. Where riverfront warehouses have survived intact they have become highly desirable. Narrow Street pioneered Docklands regeneration and warehouse living, and attracted high profile residents. Film director David Lean lived in Sun Wharf on Narrow Street, four warehouses knocked together with a basement cinema. He became something of a recluse, leaving the house less and less, and never learning how to use a telephone.

David Owen has lived on Narrow Street for 40 years, and the Limehouse Declaration of 1981 which set up the Social Democratic Party was signed at his house (notably it was not called the Ratcliff

Declaration). Although it is decades since he was Foreign Secretary, a security detail still monitors a section of the Thames foreshore near Ratcliff Cross Stairs on his behalf. The Grapes pub on Narrow Street is now owned by residents typical of the presentable, high income side of Ratcliff: newspaper proprietor Evgeny Lebedev and actor Ian McKellen.

However, only a street away from what was once Ratcliff Cross the gaping mouth of the Limehouse Link tunnel sucks in its tribute of traffic from the Highway, Butcher Row whirls like a vortex around the Royal Peculiar of St. Katharine, the Commercial Road is peppered with dereliction, and the viaduct carrying the Docklands Light Railway isolates Ratcliff from the world beyond, as the marshes once did.

The ships have gone, and because Ratcliff was built around them, their departure tore out its heart. 'Sailor Town' has almost entirely disappeared, but evidence remains of what it used to be, from the high dock wall that runs the length of Pennington Street to the buildings that survived against the odds. Seen from Ratcliff, the neighbouring towers on the Isle of Dogs look like a mirage. This is a neighbourhood shorn of the way of life that created it, but more than just a name left over on the map.

REFERENCES

1   Bethnal Green, Blackwall, Mile End New Town, Mile End Old Town, Ratcliff, Limehouse, Poplar, Spitalfields and Stratford-le-Bow

2   Maddocks, Sydney, 'Ratcliff' in *The Copartnership Herald*, Vol. III, no. 26 (April 1933)

3   Stow, John, *The Survey of London*, Everyman 1912

4   *ibid*

5   Besant, Walter, *East London*, Century Co. 1901

6   De Quincey, Thomas, *On Murder*, Oxford University Press 2006

7   *A Pictorial and Descriptive Guide to London*, Ward, Lock & Co. 1933

8   Burke, Thomas, *East of Mansion House*, Cassell 1928

9   De Quincey, Thomas, *On Murder*, Oxford University Press 2006

10   Phillips, Watts, *The Wild Tribes of London*, London 1855

11   Anon. 'Down the Highway', *East London Observer,* No.4 (10th October 1857)

12   *ibid*

13   Ewing Ritchie, J. *The Night Side of London*, William Tweedie 1857

14   Anon. 'Down the Highway', *East London Observer,* No. 4 (10th October 1857)

15   Dickens, Charles, *Our Mutual Friend*, Oxford World Classics 2008

16   *ibid*

17   Besant, Walter, *East London*, Century Co. 1901

18   *ibid*

19   Dickens, Charles (the Younger), *Dickens' Dictionary of London*, 1879

20   *ibid*

21   Booth, Charles, *Survey Into Life and Labour in London 1886-1903*, LSE Charles Booth Online Archive

22   Maddocks, Sydney, 'Ratcliff' in *The Copartnership Herald*, Vol. V, No. 58 (December 1935)

23   Céline, Louis-Ferdinand, *Guignol's Band*, New Directions 1954

24   Booth, Charles, *Survey Into Life and Labour in London 1886-1903*, LSE Charles Booth Online Archive

25   Céline, Louis-Ferdinand, *Guignol's Band*, New Directions 1954

26   Nairn, Ian, *Nairn's London*, Penguin 1966

STREATHAM SPA

The golden era for Streatham came during the first decades of the 18th century. These were high times for London's spas and pleasure gardens, and for the little-remembered Streatham Spa.

Introduction

Streatham straddles the zone, unmarked on maps, where Victorian inner London meets inter-war suburb. Mid-20th century Streatham was highly desirable with its family-sized Victorian houses, 2-mile high street (said to be the longest in Europe) and impressive selection of theatres, cinemas and clubs. Streatham had something of a heyday in the 1950s, when the flourishing High Road was symbolised by the totemic, now demolished, Pratt's department store. Streatham was a testing ground for the new consumer era. Britain's first supermarket, Express Dairies Premier Stores, opened opposite Streatham Hill Station in 1951, followed shortly afterwards by the first country's first Waitrose.

However, the settled, bustling post-war neighbourhood was barely 50 years old. Fields beyond the edge of London began to fill with houses in the late 1870s, and in the course of little more than ten years Streatham had become part of London. Previously it had been a small Surrey village strung along the Brighton Road, consisting mostly of farms and country estates; but despite its apparent insignificance it was already famous, well-known to generations of Londoners. The golden era for Streatham came during the first decades of the 18th century. These were high times for London's spas and pleasure gardens, and for the little-remembered Streatham Spa.

A spring in the woods

Traces of the Spa remain, well-hidden on the ridge above Streatham High Road. The wide grass slopes of Streatham Common climb steeply to a thick, dark treeline. The trees are a reminder of the Great North Wood which, until the Middle Ages, covered ten miles of countryside from Croydon to Dulwich. For centuries the roads south from London passed under the dark, sometimes threatening canopy of the Norwood, but the trees disappeared piece by piece. They became fuel and buildings materials for a growing London, and were even used to build ships for the Royal Navy at Deptford.

Streatham Common retains more than a hint of its former wildness. The woods crouch on a ridge overlooking the town, which hugs the valley below. Hidden in woods are the unexpected, formal gardens of the Rookery, a lost landscape of cedars, lawns, terraces, rockeries and water gardens with views to the North Downs. It is both elegant and a little odd. The gardens seem too elaborate for the modest White House, which is more of a suburban hilltop villa than a mansion. The sense of an absence here is due to the partial demolition of the house by a combination of the London County Council and the Luftwaffe, but by then a great deal had already been and gone. Norwood Grove, as the house and gardens are properly known, is the site of the original Streatham Spa.

Well in The Rookery, Streatham Common

The Rookery gardens feature a Jack-and-Jill-style well set among crazy paving and council bedding plants. It looks like a garden ornament, but a small plaque suggests otherwise: the well under the canopy is the last survivor of the three springs that gave Streatham Spa its water. In 1659 a chance discovery by labourers working on the hill "made this little village a rival to the fashionable haunts of Bath and Cheltenham",[1] according to local historian Lt.-Col. J.J. Sexby.

A strong purgative

The springs that became Streatham Spa were discovered in 1659, the year Richard Cromwell's Protectorate fell apart. Their existence was revealed when a plough-horse slipped in a muddy hollow at the top of Streatham Common, and the investigating ploughmen found a spring. Two more were later discovered nearby. Sometime later thirsty labourers, taking a break from weeding on the hill, tried the waters and, presumably to their surprise, discovered they were a powerful purgative. This was exactly what was so sought after in the 18th century, as a national obsession with taking the waters took hold.

Not long afterwards a local man, feeling ill, reportedly gave Streatham water a try after Epsom water had failed to help him. He was reported to have passed four worms, one of which was 8 feet 3 inches long, "as attested to me by several of the neighbours and the minister that saw it measured."[2] Wells were sunk to commercialise the mineral water, which contained magnesium sulphate as its main ingredient. It apparently tasted like weak sea water, with a sulphurous kick.

This was all the encouragement Londoners needed to make the trip south and purge themselves. As the Spa's popularity grew, society began to congregate. Coach queues formed along the High Road, waiting to turn beside the Common and inch to the top of the hill. Mile-long queues were, apparently, not uncommon. The surprisingly tough gradient on road to the top, where larger vehicles are still known to slide in icy weather, must have added an extra frisson to the journey.

Streatham was soon one of the most significant spas in London and the slopes of Streatham Common, with their "smooth, bright turf", became "a fashionable promenade".[3] The rural nature of the area was part of the attraction, crowds taking advantage of a day in the countryside without the need to travel far from London. By 1701 concerts were held every Monday and Thursday in the summer season, which made the crowds as "gay and frivolous as their ailments would allow".[4]

Cold, weeping, rushy clay

The first surviving description of the Spa is from John Aubrey, who included Streatham in his chaotic but illuminating history of Surrey.

To avoid the "drudgery of another transcribing" Aubrey decided
to "set some things down tumultarily, as if tumbled out of a sack."[5]
He describes Streatham as "a small scattering village about a mile in
length, and six miles from London, much frequented by the Gentry
and Citizens of that place."

He depicts the heavy South London clay from which the spring
water emerges with great accuracy: "It is a cold, weeping and rushy
clay ground". The water, Aubrey says, has a "maukish Taste… it
turns milk for a posset" (curdles milk). He claims Streatham water
was particularly powerful and that "five or six cups is the most they
drink, but the common dose around here is but three, which are held
equivalent to nine at Epsom."[6]

The water developed a reputation for a wide range of cures, including
rheumatism, gout, jaundice, bilious attacks and blindness. The three
wells also had different effects from each other, and "the middle one
does give a vomit".[7] By 1717 the waters were being bottled and sold to
London hospitals and coffee-houses, where they must have taken the
coffee drinkers who bought it as a hangover cure by surprise.

The 17th century craze for taking the waters meant that Streatham
was only one of three spas on the same South London ridge,
competing with Beulah Spa and Sydenham Wells not far away.
The facilities at Sydenham Wells, three miles to the east, consisted
of little more than a cottage and a few huts where patients lodged.
This did not, however, put off George III who spent long visits there.
Sydenham also had a less reputable side, and a doctor wrote of "a
rabble of Londoners and others frequenting these wells on Sundays,
where, under pretence of drinking of the waters, they spend that holy
day in great profaneness: who after they have gorged themselves with
the water, do drink upon it an excessive quantity of Brandy (that Bane
of Englishmen), thereby many of them becoming greatly prejudiced
in their health (to add to their folly and crime) have not been ashamed
to impute their indisposition to this Water."[8]

Beulah Spa, just over a mile to the south, had its moment in the sun later on during the 1830s, when a Decimus Burton-landscaped garden opened with lakes, a camera obscura, and views as far as Windsor Castle on a clear day. Entertainment included concerts, military bands, dancing, archery, fêtes and plenty more. In 1833, William IV's brother, the Duke of Gloucester, came by "to stimulate his jaded liver by potations".[9]

Streatham pitched its wares somewhere between the two. It relied on the qualities of its waters rather than entertainments to draw the crowds, but it seems to have remained respectable as well as popular. For better or for worse, there are no reports of the kind of exuberant behaviour seen at Sydenham.

Hermits and gypsies

Streatham is a village created as a stopping point on the main route to the coast, its name meaning 'street settlement'. The road in question, now the A23 from London to Brighton, is thought to have originally been the Roman Stane Street which led to the vanished Novus Portus, a 'new port' probably in the vicinity of modern Brighton. It is safe to say that for much of Streatham's history most people passed through, stopping out of necessity rather than choice.

During the time of the Spa, the Horse and Groom pub on Streatham High Road became a convenient official stopping-off point for stage coaches on the route to Brighton. George IV, as Prince of Wales in the 1780s and 1790s, also found it a handy stop en route to the coast, and the pub became known for gambling and cock-fighting, although this cannot be blamed entirely on the influence of the future king.

The Brighton road was the most direct route out of London to the south, but travelling through the woods proved dangerous over the course of several centuries. Frederick Arnold claimed, excitably, that the graveyard of St. Leonard's Church contained the bodies of many people buried there "found dead, foully murdered by the numerous

Horse and Groom pub, Streatham High Road

footpads who infested the roads in times gone by",[10] a claim that is more imagination that anything else. Lt.-Col. J.J. Sexby provided a more measured account: "In the latter days of the last century [the 17th century], the journey from Streatham to London, through the country, was far too dangerous to be attempted by night, unless with a strong escort, and even in the daytime the adventurous traveller had need to be fully armed."[11]

The countryside through which the old road ran was remote enough in 1545 for a hermit, Richard Adams, to set up next to the River Graveney. The river, now mostly tucked away behind houses, marks the southern border of Streatham at a street still called Hermitage Lane.[12] Centuries later, in 1802, the countryside was still wild enough to house a 'hermit': a Welshman called Samuel Matthews, known as 'Matthews the Hairyman' or 'the Wild Man of the Woods', who had absented himself from a madhouse and lived in woodland near

Dulwich College. Here he enjoyed "a pipe and a full pot of beer (for he never called for less)" with visitors.[13]

Around the same time a Dr. Leese, who lived in isolation at Central Hill on the ridge above Streatham, was in the habit of firing his pistol on dark nights "to let people know he had firearms in the house".[14] His paranoia may have been justified: the William IV pub on Hermitage Lane (demolished in the 2000s) was apparently used by robbers. It had its license removed in 1817 when "certain melting processes" were discovered being used on silver and gold watches in the blacksmith's shop next door.[15]

A story from 1792, of a baby girl found abandoned on Streatham Green and named Perdita Green by her rescuers, brings a whiff of Shakespearean otherness to what were still dark, enclosing woods. The Great North Wood was known for its gipsy encampments, as the nearby neighbourhood of Gipsy Hill recalls. Gipsies lived around the edges of built-up London in the 18th century, despite having been theoretically expelled from England in the 1560s, and the most famous encampments were at Norwood.

The gipsies drew visitors to the woods over many decades, looking for an exotic day out. Samuel Pepys wrote in 1668 that "This afternoon my wife, and Mercer, and Deb., went with Pelling to see the gypsies at Lambeth, and have their fortunes told; but what they did, I did not enquire."[16] In 1798 the artist Johan Zoffany and friends visited a gipsy family, and Zoffany later painted 'The Gypsies at Norwood'. Two hundred years later a story was told about a party of 30 Romanies led by an elderly man wearing an elaborately embroidered coat who drank in the Greyhound pub, which is still to be found at the foot of Streatham Common. When they left he paid the bill with a bag of gold and silver coins.

The Castle of Indolence

In the 18th century Streatham began to change after centuries of stability. Streatham, now easier to access from London on improved turnpike roads, was popular with businessmen building themselves country retreats, and chunks of the ancient manorial estates were sold for development. Large farms had been owned by the Manor of Tooting Bec, probably since Saxon times. The popularity of the Spa drew people to the area, including Samuel Johnson. He became closely associated with Streatham, spending a great deal of time at a new mansion built by a wealthy brewer friend, and a road across Tooting Bec Common is named Dr. Johnson's Avenue after him.

Thrale Hall was a high society beacon of the 1700s, a sizeable country house set in parkland between Tooting Bec Common and Streatham. Properly known as Streatham Park (or Place), it was owned by Johnson's close friends Henry and Hester Thrale. Henry Thrale was an MP with a fortune from his family business, the famous Anchor Brewery in Southwark.

Dr. Johnson was a particular friend of Hester Thrale, who he first met in 1765 when he was at a low ebb, suffering from the depression that periodically afflicted him. She was so alarmed at his state of health that she took him back with her to Streatham, where he remained off and on for much of the next 16 years. Although "his most ardent admirer would not call him a lover of nature",[17] Johnson would walk from the Thrales' house the mile or so along the High Road and up the hill across Streatham Common to the Spa.

An intellectual circle formed around him at Streatham Park in the 1760s and 1770s. As well as Johnson, visitors included Joshua Reynolds, who painted a series of portraits of the regular guests at the house – such luminaries as Edmund Burke, David Garrick and Oliver Goldsmith. These hung in the library and were nicknamed 'The Streatham Worthies' by Fanny Burney, a close friend of Johnson's who recorded and caricatured the era.

Women also played a significant role in the Streatham Park circle. The Blue Stockings Society was founded there in 1750 by a group of women with an interest in education and literature. It included such figures as Sophy Streatfield, apparently not only one of the most beautiful women of her time but also "the most accomplished coquette that ever breathed." She had a particular interest in tall, thin men, but "…no one of the male sex was safe from her attentions. Old and young, married and single, noblemen, reverend very reverend and even right reverend divines."[18]

Streatham Park was described by the Thrales as a villa, but was in fact a large country house with 100 acres of grounds including gravel walks, a shrubbery, a lake and drawbridge, ha-ha, kitchen gardens with 14 foot walls, and hothouses. Streatham Park "became for Johnson a Castle of Indolence."[19] The Thrales gave him his own apartment, which he described as 'home'. He also continued his life in town at his Gough Square house behind the Cheshire Cheese pub on Fleet Street, where he would go off drinking with friends on a whim at 3am "in joyous contempt of sleep".[20] At the same time he lived a parallel fantasy existence as an adopted family member in Streatham, which made him happy but also seemed to prevent him from writing.

This happy time came to an end with Henry Thrale's death in 1781, and Streatham Park was let out to the short-lived Whig Prime Minister, the Earl of Shelburne. He used it for negotiations with France over the Peace of Paris, which ended the American War of Independence. He also, apparently, caused a great deal of damage and returned the house in a poor state.

Hester Thrale's account of a wedding anniversary dinner shows the scale on which Streatham Park operated. It also suggests a prickly relationship with the people of Streatham: "At Night the Trees & Front of the House were illuminated with Colour'd Lamps, that called forth our Neighbours from all the adjacent Villages to admire & enjoy such Diversion… no less than a Thousand Men Women & Children might have been counted in the House & Grounds, where tho' all were admitted, nothing was stolen, lost, broken, or even damaged – a Circumstance almost incredible."[21]

Thrale Hall was demolished in 1863. A visitor immediately prior to the demolition reported that 18th century wig pegs could still be seen in the rooms used by Dr. Johnson. The Streatham Park council estate now occupies the site, but the mature trees still standing among the houses are reminders of the Thrales' park.

The Spa lives on

Remarkably enough Streatham waters were still on sale during the first half of the 20th century but by this time the source had changed. The original Spa was closed to the public in 1792, probably because the water had become contaminated. By 1913, when the gardens of Norwood Grove opened as a public park after a local campaign, only one of the original three wells remained. However, another set of springs had been fortuitously discovered further down the hill, and they came to replace the original Spa.

The new well was on Valley Road, halfway down the slope towards Streatham High Road, in a neighbourhood still called Streatham Wells. It was on land that had been part of the now lost Leigham (or Lime) Common. A wide stretch of open ground between modern Hill House Road and Leigham Court Road, it was notoriously water-logged, its clay used for tile-making, but by 1816 it had been enclosed as fields.

The Well House, still standing on Well Close, was built in the early 1780s to bottle the spring water. Here water was pumped, sold, and distributed until the Second World War. This was more of a local enterprise than the first Streatham Spa, and attracted fewer visitors from outside the area. The spa era was ending, and London spas were all in terminal decline. Streatham Wells, as it became known, had nowhere for visitors to stay nor much in the way of entertainment, although there was a tea garden where they could drink glasses of the water at a penny a time.

Streatham's convenience, once its main attraction, was no longer a selling point for a public able to travel further afield. The Quaker author Priscilla Wakefield wrote in 1809 that the spa "would probably be more highly esteemed for its medicinal qualities by Londoners if it was not so near home, as the water is sent in considerable quantities to the hospitals",[22] which gives an insight into the 16th century nature of the medical treatment on offer at the time.

Streatham Wells (still the name of the local council ward) continued to sell the waters and draw in custom throughout the 19th century. An advertisement from 1895 quotes the results of chemical analysis at the wells, which concluded that "it is not unpleasant to the taste; on the contrary, it leaves behind it a freshness which is grateful to the palate."[23] The water was still in enough demand to be exported "to all parts of the United Kingdom" and, for reasons that are now obscure, to Buenos Aires and to Delagoa Bay (on the coast of Mozambique).[24] However, by 1910 Alfred Foord reported that "There is now scarcely any local sale for the water, but the attendant who dispenses the fluid states that she drinks a glass of this water every morning."[25]

By this time, the business had expanded and Streatham Wells had become the Curtis Brothers Dairy. The business was upgraded in 1926 to become the Curtis and Dumbrill Dairy bottling plant. A postcard shows off the resplendent mock Tudor offices, now sadly disappeared. New brick industrial units and a substantial chimney stack show they meant business. The complex featured a model dairy, with a viewing window for the public to marvel at the new automated bottling line.

Streatham water remained available for delivery with the milk until the Second World War. The dairy survived into the 2000s, by which time it was owned by Unigate, but was replaced by housing during 2014. The unromantically named Unigate Woods behind are a remaining fragment of the lost Leigham Common, and contain a seasonal stream that rises from the hillside.

Streatham Common South

   Streatham Wells was far from the only active spring in the village.
Springs can still be found on the hillside, and the steep side roads
still experience spontaneous leaks and floods. Down in the valley at
No.27 Streatham High Road, near Streatham Hill Station, there was
a building called The Pump House where a pure water spring was
discovered in 1736. Although it had no pretensions to cure anything,
the pump was maintained by the parish and the water delivered
in buckets by the postman, who operated a pony and cart with an
outsized barrel perched on top. This service was available until the
1880s. The Pump House was eventually demolished in 1936, replaced
by one of the art deco pre-War flats that now characterise Streatham
High Road.

Streatham after the Spa

Streatham Hill Station still looks like the country halt it was when it first opened in 1856, serving no more than a ribbon of buildings along the High Road. Twenty years later Streatham had been repurposed from village to high class suburb: a Victorian Metroland served by the London, Brighton and South Coast railway and occupied by the newly expanded middle class, from city clerks to senior government officials. The streets were filled with elaborate red-brick semi-detached villas, with an English freestyle combination of Eastern fantasy copper domes and cupolas, bucolic terracotta friezes, and country vicarage porches.

By the end of the 19th century Streatham had moved a long way from the days of country houses and the Spa, now firmly tied to urban London rather than rural Surrey. Its new identity is reflected by Arthur Conan Doyle, who lived in nearby South Norwood during the 1890s. He sent Sherlock Holmes to various leafy parts of South London where the suburban mansions of respectable men with shameful secrets were to be found. The action in 'The Beryl Coronet' centres on a house in Streatham called 'Fairbank', the "modest residence of the great financier" Arthur Holder, where Holmes prevents a "great, public scandal"[26] in the nick of time.

'Fairbank' seems to have been based on Streatham Lodge, now demolished, which was at the foot of Streatham Common.[27] It was in reality the home of Matthew Coulthurst, a Senior Partner at Coutts Bank for much of the 1800s, representative of the professionals who now lived in Streatham. Their lifestyles were scaled-down in comparison with the Thrales', but still remarkable. After Coulthurst's death in 1898, the house sale included "200 dozens of old wines and spirits", 4,000 cigars, cabinets of birds' eggs, corals, sponges and shells, and a marble bust of the Duke of Wellington, as well as the contents of the farm that occupied the surrounding fields.

Streatham was badly hit not only by Second World War bombs,

but also by a Zeppelin raid in 1916. The damage caused by the airship, whose pilot threw out bombs by hand, is preserved in brick: the 'Broadway' nameplate on a Victorian shopping parade at No.322 Streatham High Road, sheared in half by a bomb blast, remains as a miniature memorial. However, the list of victims provides a snapshot of the still-desirable Streatham suburbs of the early 20th century. Houses hit included those of Belgrave Ninnis, Royal Navy Inspector General, distinguished surgeon and Arctic explorer, and Frederick Palmer, proprietor of *The Church Times*.

However, the ordered nature of a respectable suburb generates oppositional forces, and Streatham is no exception. Dennis Wheatley, superstar horror novelist, lived for his first 25 years in houses beside the High Road in the vicinity of Streatham Hill, before reinventing himself with a flat in Knightsbridge. At the other end of a High Road axis, Aleister Crowley lived in a house near Streatham Common with his intensely religious mother. According to the notoriously unreliable Crowley's own account, while at school in Streatham he built a homemade rocket fuelled with gunpowder which exploded on lift-off, breaking windows along the High Road. Raymond Chandler also spent an incongruous couple of years living in Streatham Hill while in his teens, attending Dulwich College.

Since the demise of the Spa, Streatham has steadily become less of a place to be noticed and more a part of the south London spread. A combination of general anonymity and a handy main road even made Streatham the location until the mid-2000s of MI5's garage, housed in a shabby industrial building with a suspiciously sophisticated security system (at the junction with Kempshott Road, now demolished). Streatham's 21st century status as a place to disappear was also underlined by the case of the Streatham warlord. Afghan refugee Faryadi Zardad came to London fleeing the Taliban in 1996, and lived for a time in Gleneagle Road, a central Streatham street of flats and bedsits. However, as revealed at his Old Bailey trial in 2005, he had previously been a mujahideen commander controlling the main road from Kabul to Jalalabad and using particular savagery, including employing a 'human dog' to maul prisoners.

Streatham, now a place of comings and goings and still somewhere to avoid attention, is almost unrecognisable from its days as a rural spa. The time when Streatham was a name known in Buenos Aires may have gone for good, but the modern suburb was shaped by the Spa. Traces of its previous incarnation help us to picture an unlikely existence from a pre-modern rural past.

REFERENCES

1   Sexby, Lt.-Col. J.J. *History of Streatham Common*, Local History Reprints 1991

2   Brown, John W. *Aubrey's History of Streatham*, Local History Reprints, 1989

3   Foord, A.S. *Springs, Streams and Spas of London*, T. Fisher Unwin 1910

4   Sexby, Lt.-Col. J.J. *History of Streatham Common*, Local History Reprints 1991

5   Brown, John W. *Aubrey's History of Streatham*, Local History Reprints 1989

6   *ibid*

7   *ibid*

8   Sunderland, S.P. *Old London's Spas and Wells*, John Bale Sons and Danielsson Ltd. 1915

9   *ibid*

10   Arnold, F. *History of Streatham*, Elliot Stock 1888

11   Sexby, Lt.-Col. J.J. *History of Streatham Common*, Local History Reprints 1991

12   Brown, John W., Brewer, Roger A., David, Cecil T., *A Chronology of the Parish of Streatham*, Local History Publications 2007

13   *The life of Samuel Matthews, the Norwood Hermit*, etc., N.D. (copy in Minet Public Library)

14   Saward, Arthur A. *Reminiscences of Norwood* 1907 (copy in Minet Public Library)

15   Baldwin, Herbert, *Streatham Old and New*, Local History Reprints 1993

16   Pepys, Samuel, *The Diary of Samuel Pepys* Vol. 9. 1668-9. University of California Press 1995

17   Sexby, Lt.-Col. J.J. *History of Streatham Common*, Local History Reprints 1991

18   Grant, Lt.-Col F. *The Life of Dr Johnson,* Walter Scott 1887

19   *ibid*

20   Boswell, James, *The Life of Samuel Johnson*, Penguin 2008

21   Piozzi, Hester Lynch, ed. Balderston, Katherine C. *Thraliana*, Clarendon Press, Oxford 1942

22   Foord, A.S. *Springs, Streams and Spas of London*, T. Fisher Unwin 1910

23   *ibid*

24   *ibid*

25   *ibid*

26   Conan Doyle, Sir Arthur, *The Adventures of Sherlock Holmes*, Penguin 2007

27   Brown, John W. *Sherlock Holmes in Streatham*, Local History Publications 1993

WELLCLOSE: THE FORGOTTEN EAST END

It is almost impossible to guess that the Shadwell estates now sandwiched between the Commercial Road and The Highway were, until not long ago, a distinctive dockland neighbourhood centred on two elegant 17th century squares.

Introduction

Wellclose is a lost neighbourhood that requires more tracing than most. Largely through the kind of post-war reconstruction only attempted in poorer parts of London, it has been all but erased from the map. It is almost impossible to guess that the Shadwell estates now sandwiched between the Commercial Road and The Highway were, until not long ago, a distinctive dockland neighbourhood centred on two elegant 17th century squares. Their logic has been fractured and scattered, and Wellclose is hemmed in by unendingly busy roads. Only the aloof, pepperpot tower of St. George-in-the-East draws a second glance. Yet behind its dilapidated and somewhat forbidding surface, Wellclose is a place with an independent and sometimes bizarre history waiting to be rediscovered.

The Liberty

The Liberty of Wellclose was one of a handful of tiny territories belonging to the Tower of London, all of which operated for several centuries as semi-independent enclaves. Other Tower Liberties were East Smithfield and The Minories, adjacent to the Tower's walls. Wellclose was a little further east, linked to St. Mary Grace's Abbey which was founded in 1350 and apparently known as 'Eastminster'. Grace's Alley, off Wellclose Square, is the only remaining indication that Wellclose was once part of the Abbey grounds. When the monasteries were dissolved in the 1530s and the Abbey demolished, the Tower Liberties remained outside the control of the judicial system. James II confirmed the special status of the Liberty of Wellclose in 1688. Law and order in the liberties was maintained by the Governor of the Tower who had his own magistrates, and was permitted to put offenders on trial for any crime, including treason.

The special status of London's liberties was finally abolished in 1855 when they were subsumed into their surrounding parishes. However, the bounds of the Liberty of Wellclose were still beaten every Ascension Day until 1897 to mark the territory, by a procession of boys, sons of soldiers serving at the Tower of London. They wore red, white and blue ribbons and carried willow wands and were led by the Lieutenant of the Tower. The boundaries of the Tower itself are still beaten today in the same way, but the Liberties are no longer included.

Scandinavian squares

The main feature of Wellclose is two large squares: Wellclose Square (originally called Marine Square) and Swedenborg Square (originally Prince's Square). Wellclose Square still exists although its shape is now hard to discern, one side blocked off by Shapla Primary School. Swedenborg Square is now called Swedenborg Gardens and is dominated by the three tower blocks of the St. George's Estate. The two squares were products of the post-Fire rebuilding and expansion of the City of London. They were laid out gradually, beginning in 1678, in fields beside the Ratcliff Highway, the main road from the City to the ships berthed at Ratcliff [see 'Ratcliff: Sailor Town' chapter].

The development was built by Nicholas Barbon, an early free market philosopher and the original speculative London developer. The son of Praise-God Barebone, an extreme Puritan Civil War politician, he possessed the surely unique middle name of If-Jesus-Christ-Had-Not-Died-For-Thee-Thou-Hadst-Been-Damned. He was known for his aggressive attitude to business and did not let small matters, such as whether or not he owned the land he planned to develop, hold him back. He was responsible for many of the new houses which sprang up in Bloomsbury and Covent Garden after the 1666 Fire, linking the City of London and the City of Westminster for the first time.

Their proximity to the Docks meant that the new squares were handy for merchants and ships' captains who needed to commute to the East London wharves around Limehouse and Ratcliff. The two squares were spacious and respectable, much more civilised than the crowded, ramshackle hamlets by the Thames. From the early 1600s the stretch of Cable Street at Wellclose was known as 'Knockfergus', a reference to the Irish emigrants who fled there during the Nine-Years War, the Gaelic Irish rebellion against Elizabeth I in the 1590s, and the famine that followed.

The timber trade also brought Scandinavian ships and merchants to London, and they made Wellclose their home. A Danish church was built in the centre of Marine Square in 1694, designed by Danish architect Caius Gabriel Cibber and paid for by the King of Denmark. Cibber also designed a series of iconic London sculptures, including the statue of Charles II that still stands in the middle of Soho Square;

the stone reliefs around the base of the Monument; and the statues of Melancholy and Raving Madness, now lost, which guarded the entrance to Bedlam. A smaller Swedish chapel was built in the centre of Prince's Square in 1729, named the Ulrika Leanora after an 18th century Swedish queen.

Marine Square was large and enclosed, with a peculiar design that included distinctive, narrow alleyways at each corner. Just one, Grace's Alley, survives. Wellclose Street and Fletcher Street, two more original access streets, have had their names changed and have lost all their buildings, but just about still exist.

Prince's Square was the more modest of the two, built on a slightly reduced scale with less open space in the middle. It was the centre of Swedish life in London for much of the 19th century and the most famous Swede of the time, 'The Swedish Nightingale' Jenny Lind, attended the chapel here. There is little now to suggest the square was ever there at all and only Swedenborg Gardens, a road running along one side of the original square, now remains of the street pattern. Stockholm House, one of the three tower blocks of the St. George's Estate, stands in what was once the middle of Prince's Square, on the site of the Swedish Chapel.

The Scandinavians eventually moved away, and the Danish Church was demolished in 1869, its congregation having dwindled. A replacement Danish church, St. Katharine, was set up near Regent's Park where it still operates and the fixtures and fittings from the old church were taken there. St. Paul's School was built in its place, and its weathervane – a gilded ship – was taken from another church, St. Paul's Church for Seamen, in nearby Dock Road.

The Swedish Chapel lasted longer, closing in 1911 and moving to Marylebone. The building was knocked down in 1921, but the font is now in Swedenborg Gardens where it was placed in 1960 to commemorate the 250th anniversary of the Ulrika Leonora.

Ulrika Leonora Church memorial, Swedenborg Gardens

The occult squares

Wellclose Square has acquired an unlikely reputation and has been described as "one of London most historically significant occult locations."[1] Part of the theory involves hidden patterns within Christopher Wren's plans for a new London after the Great Fire. The Bible contains dimensions for a New Jerusalem, set out in the Book of Numbers, and occult writers claim that Wren's plans were based on these. St. Paul's Cathedral is supposedly 2,000 cubits (forearm lengths) from the eastern and western boundaries of the City of London, and Wellclose Square the same distance from the City's edge, with Nicholas Hawksmoor's Christ Church Spitalfields the same distance again from Wellclose Square.

Hawksmoor himself has collected a posthumous occult reputation in London literature and another of his churches, St. George-in-the-

East beside Swedenborg Gardens, is built in a particularly unsettling English Baroque – a "drug addict's dream"[2] – which still holds its own beside the thundering traffic of the Ratcliff Highway. It is easy to read hidden purposes into the church, the confrontational strangeness of its design lacking any surface rationale. All Hawksmoor's London churches have a similar feeling of hallucinatory otherness, and St. George-in-the-East seems to prefigure the new East End that was just around the corner when they were built, a place of new urban sensation and horror.

No occult picture would be complete without Jack the Ripper, who has connections to Wellclose. In 1888 Sven Olsson lived at 33 Prince's Square and was the clerk at the Swedish Chapel. He was a friend of Liz Stride, Swedish-born (her maiden name was Gustafsdotter) and known as 'Long Liz'. Despite help from Olsson, Stride had been a prostitute for many years and worked the streets of the East End. Her body was discovered early in the morning of 30th September 1888, throat cut, in a yard off what is now Henriques Street, just north of Wellclose. Her body was taken to the mortuary at St. George-in-the-East, where Olsson identified her. Her murder was the first of two on the same night, and the next day the police received the famous 'Saucy Jacky' postcard which claimed responsibility for the "double event" and was signed "Jack the Ripper".

Swedenborg in exile

The occult reputation of Wellclose, however, does not just rely on its strange church. Two 18th century residents also cast long shadows. Swedenborg Square was renamed in tribute to Emanuel Swedenborg, who lodged there when he came to London in 1766. Swedenborg was a remarkable man, already 65 by the time he left Sweden, whose genius led him to a series of scientific discoveries that were years ahead of their time. During his scientific career in Sweden he invented a flying machine and a submarine; became an expert in smelting; ran Sweden's mines; discovered the neuron; and spent his spare time on astronomy, book-binding, chemistry, geometry, mathematics, philosophy, physics, poetry and watch-making. However, he is mostly remembered for his sudden transformation into a mystic Christian visionary.

In 1745 he had been troubled by strange dreams for some time. While having dinner in a private room at a London inn, a strange man suddenly appeared in the corner and spoke, warning him not to eat too much. Swedenborg reported that "Towards the end of the meal I noticed a kind of blurring in my vision, it grew dark and I saw the floor covered with the nastiest crawling animals, like snakes, frogs, and creatures of that kind. I was amazed, because I was fully conscious and thinking clearly. After a while the prevailing darkness was quickly dispelled, and I saw a man sitting in the corner of the room." In subsequent appearances the strange man revealed himself to be God, and showed Swedenborg how the Bible should be interpreted.

This vision changed everything, and Swedenborg spent the rest of his life writing theological works and travelling between Stockholm, the Netherlands and Wellclose Square, where he stayed at a Swedish-owned pub called the King's Arms. According to the landlord, Eric Bergstrom, he "dressed in velvet, breakfasted on coffee, took a daily morning walk, lunched moderately with one or two glasses of wine, never ate supper, retired early… He was kind, generous and always agreeable, but somewhat reserved."[3]

The more liberal censorship regime in Britain allowed him to publish work denounced as heresy in Sweden, although people seemed as much baffled as offended. His unconventional ideas were based around the idea that there is correspondence between the physical world and another, higher, spiritual world. He claimed that the Last Judgement was over, having already taken place in 1759 in the World of Spirits, located halfway between heaven and hell. He was revered and also feared, and stories circulated of his psychic powers.

Swedenborg died aged 84 in 1772 having correctly predicted the

"True Charity is the desire to be useful to others without thought of recompense"
Emanuel Swedenborg

Swedenborg Gardens, off Ratcliff Highway

day of his death in a letter to John Wesley a few weeks before. He was buried in the Swedish Chapel in Prince's Square, which was named after him in 1938. His visions heavily influenced William Blake, who visited the first Swedenborgian Church when it opened in London in 1789, and also many later writers including W.B. Yeats.

When the Swedish Chapel closed in 1911, the Swedish Navy sent a warship to repatriate his remains. However, his skull famously went missing en route. The story is murky, but the captain of the warship that collected his body was a keen phrenologist, and is alleged to have stolen it for his collection. Another sailor then stole the skull he had substituted. The fake skull was retrieved from the sailor, years later, by the pastor of the Swedish Chapel. The real skull, however, went on a 150-year journey via an antique shop in Wales, before resurfacing at Sotheby's in 1978 when it was reunited with the rest of Swedenborg. There are several versions of this story, however, and it may be that, like the missing skull of Ratcliff Highway murderer John Williams which disappeared from the same area [see 'Ratcliff: Sailor Town' chapter], it vanished into "London's cabinet of curiosities".[4]

The London Baal Shem

The other inhabitant of Wellclose Square credited with supernatural powers was Rabbi Chaim Falk. He arrived in London in 1742, hotfoot from Westphalia, where he had been condemned to burn to death for sorcery. Falk was an adept of the Cabbala – a Baal Shem, or 'Master of the Name' – who knew the secret names of God. The knowledge was supposed to bring with it the ability to work miracles, and Falk was reputed to have, at various times, survived for six weeks without food or drink, stopped a fire in its tracks by writing Hebrew letters on a door, commanded the wheel that had fallen off his carriage to follow him home, and used his magic to do the housework. Falk was also alleged to have cursed Elias Levy, the previous owner of his Wellclose Square house, who died suddenly shortly after they fell out.

He practised as an alchemist from a laboratory on Prescot Street near London Bridge, which he decked out in Cabbalistic paraphernalia. Arriving in London a penniless refugee, he did so well that he was able to afford a large and handsome house at Wellclose Square, but this may have had more to do with his pawnbroking business than his alchemy.

At Wellclose Square, Falk became a figure of repute, and was visited by famous characters of the time including Casanova, who was probably interested in his experiments in achieving continuous orgasm through Cabbalistic sex magic. Theodor von Neuhoff, an adventurer who had briefly been King of Corsica, also visited in the hope that alchemy could pay for him to take the island back. After Falk died in 1782, rumours grew that he had buried a stash of treasure and other precious objects in Epping Forest, but it has yet to be found.

Slaves and masters

The two new squares were never quite as respectable as Nicholas Barbon had intended. The houses, although handsome, were surrounded by mixed, haphazardly planned streets. A combination of industrial premises and lodging houses and taverns that served the Docks grew up, surrounding Wellclose on all sides. Ropewalks, where rope was manufactured, occupied much of the remaining undeveloped land and the area also became known for its glassworks. Dock Street was previously called Saltpetre Bank, named after one of the main materials used in the glassmaking process.

From early on Wellclose gathered a poor reputation, a taint that never went away. Daniel Defoe, writing in 1724, reported that "Well Close, now called Marine Square, was so remote from houses, that it used to be a very dangerous place to go over after it was dark, and many people have been robbed and abused in passing it; a well standing in the middle, just where the Danish church is now built, there the mischief was generally done."[5]

However, merchants still lived in the houses even if the neighbourhood was rough and ready. The poet Thomas Day was born in Wellclose Square in 1748. He is best known as the author of 'The Dying Negro', very popular in its day, which is written as the suicide note of a slave captured while trying to elope with a white woman. This was not an entirely fictional scenario among the slave-owning merchants of Wellclose, as a 1761 newspaper advertisement demonstrates:

RUN AWAY FROM CAPTAIN STUBBS. Yellowish Negro Man, about Five Feet Seven Inches, a very flat Nose, and a Scar above his Forehead, he had when he run away, a white Pea-Jacket, a pair of black Worsted Stockings, and a black Wig. Whoever will bring the said Negro Man to his above-mentioned Master, Capt. Stubbs in Prince's Square, Ratcliffe-highway, shall receive Two Guineas Reward.[6]

Wellclose Square did not just consist of houses: it had its own gaol, handy for captured runaways, but mostly used to incarcerate debtors. The Wellclose Prison was on Neptune Street (now Wellclose Street) under the Cock and Neptune pub. The pub's landlord was also the gaoler, and the prison was run as a commercial operation, with people encouraged to come and go to boost takings. A visitor in 1777 reported that several of the men in the gaol had just dropped in for a game of skittles. Because Wellclose was a liberty the prison also had its own courthouse attached, on the corner of Neptune Street and Wellclose Square. It survived into the 20th century, used first as a German club and then as a paintworks. The interior of one of the cells has been preserved in the Museum of London, the wooden walls carved with the graffiti of the prisoners, including pleas for charity and bad poetry.

As well as the gaol and courthouse, the square contained two sugar houses, which were small-scale factories where sugar was refined. In fact, Wellclose was a centre for sugar houses run by Germans during the early 1800s, with 21 separate premises recorded in the surrounding streets. No. 48 and No. 49 Wellclose Square were operated by a firm called Pritzler, Engell, Martineau & Henrickson until 1851. Afterwards, the site was taken over by George Whybrow and Sons, who made pickles, sauces and oils including "Whybrow's Popular 'Relish'" which was advertised as having "a sharp piquant flavour", and was sold in "neatly-got-up bottles".

Theatreland East

The most obvious relic of the original Wellclose Square is a single surviving corner, on Grace's Alley, which consists of a row of 19th century terraced houses and includes Wilton's Music Hall. Wilton's is the oldest remaining music hall in the country, dating from 1858 when the previous premises – the Prince of Denmark pub – was bought by John Wilton and expanded by knocking four houses together. The entrance lobby still encloses the cobbled courtyard of the original Prince of Denmark. The theatre was active for a relatively short time, rebuilt after a fire in 1877, but closed by 1880. The other three corners of the square were demolished in the 1960s, but plans to build another tower block were abandoned when it was agreed that Wilton's should be preserved. After closure it was used as a Methodist Mission Hall, and then as a rag warehouse until after the Second World War. The notorious, banned video for Frankie Goes to Hollywood's 'Relax' was shot here in 1983, and it is the favoured location for almost every Victorian drama. The building has clung on precariously, despite major structural problems with its papier-mâché interior and alarmingly thin barley sugar columns. Long-awaited restoration is finally underway.

An earlier theatre, the Royalty, was located in nearby Well Street (now Ensign Street). It opened in 1786 and was run by a man called John 'Plausible' Palmer. He apparently chose the location, just inside the boundary of the Liberty of Wellclose, in the belief that he would be free to stage plays without a licence. He was wrong, and magistrates fined him and his partner £100 each. The theatre then had a chaotic history, in the hands of dubious speculators, and burned down in 1826.

It was replaced with a new theatre, unfortunately remembered for all the wrong reasons. The Royal Brunswick Theatre opened to the public on 25th February 1828. However, the theatre's owners had ignored warnings from builders and carpenters that the new experimental iron roof could not support the weight of the stage flies hung from it. There were signs that the structure was moving in the days after opening, and three days later the roof collapsed during a rehearsal, killing 15 people and injuring 20. Charles Dickens wrote a detailed account of the tragedy, describing how "The roof came down; an avalanche of iron instantly tore walls and gallery down with it, and swept before it scenes, stage, orchestra, boxes, and actors. It was a tornado of girders, bricks, and timbers."[7] Bollards can still be seen on Ensign Street, marked with the initials 'RBT'. The Brunswick Maritime Establishment was built on the site and is still there, a three-storey building converted into flats. A sailors' home, opened in 1835 with room for 500 men, it had impressive facilities including a savings bank and reading rooms. It was designed to persuade sailors to avoid disreputable lodging houses, many of which were found along nearby Ratcliff Highway.

Forging a living

The Docks were the reason most people lived in Wellclose and the surrounding streets, but they provided an uncertain living. William Smith and Charles Eaton, known as Billy and Charley, were in many ways typical of the Wellclose population clinging on at the margins, scraping a living as mudlarks searching the Thames foreshore for objects to sell. In other ways they were rather extraordinary. Although always described as 'boys', they were in their twenties when they decided in 1857 to make their own antiquities rather than combing the mud for them. They set up a primitive casting process and flooded the market with transparently forged antiquities, complete with meaningless combinations of letters (neither could read) and childish representations of kings and saints. They produced mainly lead pilgrim medals, but also branched out into more elaborate objects including statuettes and small shrines, all of which they claimed to have found in Shadwell Dock. Many were bought by a dealer on the City Road and they were soon in wide circulation, becoming known as 'Billys and Charleys'.

Most qualified experts saw through the deception, but some argued they must be genuine on the basis that no forger would produce anything so bizarre. Despite an 1858 court case which proved their medals were fakes, dealers continued to buy and Billy and Charley carried on supplying them. Eventually their methods became too well known, but they were still operating ten years later. Neither was ever

Wilton's Music Hall, Grace's Alley

prosecuted because it was not clear whether what they were doing was actually illegal. Billy eventually disappeared from the records, but Charles Eaton died of consumption in 1879 while living in Wellclose Square. The two are thought to have produced 10,000 forgeries and they made a large amount of money, but both appear to have spent it.

Tiger Bay

From the mid-19th century until the First World War, the East End developed a notoriety that was based on the levels of poverty around the Docks, and on the sailors from all parts of the world who landed here and enjoyed themselves in the vicinity of Wellclose and the Ratcliff Highway.

Both London and the Docks were expanding very fast and conditions deteriorated as people flooded into the East End.

Overcrowding, unemployment, malnourishment, disease and alcoholism were common. In 1841 Wellclose Square was an artisan neighbourhood with 150 inhabitants. By 1861 more than 400 people lived in the same houses, including many Irish dock workers. No.47 was home to 12 German sugar refinery workers, while a 'Jews' Asylum' at No.51 housed a matron, two servants and 15 elderly Jewish men.

Wellclose Square was separated from the London Docks by no more than the width of the Highway, which was dominated by vast warehouses, basins and jetties, dwarfing the residential neighbourhood next door. A lifebuoy maker lived at No.4 in the 1840s, but local institutions such as the Destitute Sailors' Asylum on Wells Street (now Ensign Street) illustrate all too clearly the precarious, casual labour on offer to most. On Betts Street, a 'Refuge and Receiving Home' rescued 'girls and children' who were abused or pregnant, while the Naval and Military Orphans Society was based in Wellclose Square itself.

The grim realities were coloured and embellished by journalists [see 'Ratcliff: Sailor Town' chapter]. Contemporary accounts tended to take a moral standpoint, focusing on the behaviour of women, as in this 1857 description of the Wellclose neighbourhood: "an infernal hole, whole streets teeming with houses of infamy, houses not long built for the industrial classes now let out at a more profitable rent for the pursuit of sinful pleasures... [the vicar] reports that he has helped in rescuing 270 women from their degradation, yet their places are immediately filled by others... in the summer nights, it is a common thing to see large groups of bared-headed women dancing in a circle with language and attitudes so offensive as to excite pity and shame."[8]

However, the promised horrors often proved elusive. A writer called James Greenwood showed up on the Ratcliff Highway in 1874 looking for 'Tiger Bay', supposedly a nickname the area was given because of its savagery (Cardiff still has a Tiger Bay in its own former docklands). He visited a series of pubs in search of the 'tigresses', who were supposed to belong to "a race of rapacious robbers and man-catchers with an ogre-like appetite for the flesh and blood of sailors."[9] All he found was people drinking, dancing and trying to sell their coats for more brandy. He describes the experience as "like being 'behind the scenes' at the pantomime", which strongly implies he was expecting a performance.

By this time, Wellclose had become known for its exotic mix of sailors, who spent their shore leave in the neighbourhood because it was the nearest place to their ships, moored in the London Docks. Some put down roots, and Dutch, German and Irish populations arrived in place of the original Scandinavian émigrés, who seem to have largely moved away from Wellclose Square by mid-19th century, although their churches remained. The Prussian Eagle, in Ship Alley (at the south-east corner of Wellclose Square), was an infamous German pub catering to the German employees of the sugar refineries nearby. An 1872 article claimed that there was a notice at the door reading "All persons are requested, before entering the dancing saloon, to leave at the bar their pistols and knives, or any other weapon they may have about them."[10]

Remarkably enough, a real tiger features in the history of Wellclose. Charles Jamrach ran a business importing and exporting exotic animals, which arrived at London Docks and were transported to his menagerie on Betts Street and to Jamrach's Animal Emporium on Ratcliff Highway. One day in 1857, while Jamrach was dealing with some leopards, a full-grown Bengal tiger broke out of its cage on to Betts Street. A passing nine-year-old boy tried to stroke it, and it seized him in its jaws. Jamrach wrestled the tiger to the ground in a headlock, and eventually managed to rescue the boy, virtually unharmed, with the help of a crowbar. Jamrach was affronted when the boy's father later sued him for damages, although it is possible to see the father's point of view.

Sensationalist though he was, when James Greenwood returned to the area a decade later even he had to admit that 'Tiger Bay' was no longer "one of the most notorious strongholds of vice and ruffianism to be found through the length and breadth of the metropolis."[11] What once excited him now seemed merely depressing. Ship Alley was dreary and cheerless, full of "dismal-looking Prussian and Dutch beer-bars".[12] The Brigantine pub on Ratcliff Highway featured a shabby singer wearing a grubby dress and a busby, a bad pianist and a group of men sharing a single beer. He was also disappointed to find that a dance hall near Wellclose Square was no longer notorious for fights or for "painted and bedizened girls and women with naked shoulders and visible insteps".[13]

If the entertainment was no longer as wild, the poverty was getting worse. Oscar Wilde's Dorian Gray, seized with self-loathing, abased himself in the worst place he could find, which was the notorious Bluegate Fields next to St. George-in-the-East: "He would creep out of the house, go down to dreadful places near Blue Gate Fields, and stay there, day after day, until he was driven away."[14] In his 1907 novel *Ghetto Comedies*, Israel Zangwill describes a family staying the night in a cellar on Ship Alley: "It was pitch black. They say there is a hell. This may or may not be, but more of a hell than the night we passed in this cellar one does not require. Every vile thing in the world seemed to have taken up its abode therein. We sat the whole night sweeping the vermin from us."[15]

The notes taken by Charles Booth as he surveyed the streets of Wellclose fit the story. Mayfield Buildings, which was between Prince's Square and Cable Street, was "The worst place in the subdivision, not a male in the street above school age that has not been convicted. Thieves, prostitutes, rough Cockney Irish. Broken dirty windows. Bareheaded women." He described it as "a black spot", and "the ruin of Prince's Square, a quiet country-like place",[16] although the rest of the neighbourhood is classified as "mixed – some comfortable, others poor."

Post-war Wellclose

The London Docks and their neighbourhoods suffered heavier bomb damage than anywhere else in Britain, but the post-war demolition that destroyed most of Swedenborg and Wellclose Squares was not a result of bomb damage. Before the war had ended, plans were already drawn up for the reconstruction of Stepney and Poplar, and the area around Wellclose had been designated as 'Neighbourhood 5', zoned for new residential development to replace run-down housing categorised as slums.

The London Docks at Wapping, and St. Katharine's Docks next door, were too small to be efficient or to handle the larger ships now plying the trade routes, and were in terminal decline. The area around Wellclose started to shed its population, as people moved away from battered inner London after the war, and its infrastructure disappeared too. Leman Street, the station closest to Wellclose Square, closed in 1941 and its buildings were demolished in 1955.

Photographs taken at the end of the war show the western sides of both squares: substantial three-storey Georgian terraced houses, apparently suffering only blast damage. The houses in Swedenborg Square have lost doors and windows but are structurally intact, while in Wellclose Square the damage seems to amount to little more than broken windows. At the south-west corner of Wellclose Square there is also a smaller, wooden, two-storey house from the mid-18th century. It is a house from the days when London was built from wood not brick, and inhabits the black and white picture like a lingering ghost from a pre-photography era.

The squares were hanging on, but their days were numbered. Evidence of superficial damage was all that London County Council needed to decide that the squares should be cleared. Although some

Bascule Bridge, Glamis Road

houses were listed, and Grace's Alley was left untouched because of Wilton's Music Hall, most of the buildings were left to decay. This process of reconstructing the neighbourhood took 30 dispiriting years, and for much of the time people carried on living in the houses the authorities had declared unfit. Compulsory purchases were eventually made in 1959, and 76 families were moved out of the neighbourhood. In 1961 a public inquiry ruled in favour of clearing the squares for new estates.

Iain Nairn, visiting in 1966, correctly predicted the fate of both squares: "The hopeless fragments of two once splendid squares, Wellclose and Swedenborg, built for the shipmasters of Wapping when London began to move east… Nobody cares enough and the whole place will soon be a memory."[17] The fate of the Wellclose area exemplifies the way the East End was treated after Second World

War. Bomb damage in more fashionable, visible neighbourhoods was quickly repaired, but Wellclose was associated only with poverty and decay, and the chance to sweep up the remains of a once notorious neighbourhood seemed too good to miss.

The high profile local parish priest, Father Joe Williamson, played a central role in the demolition of the squares and of many other streets in the Stepney area. Born in poverty in Poplar, he became the priest at St. Paul's Dock Street, next to Wellclose Square, in 1952. He was a campaigning clergyman, known for what he called 'The Work' which consisted of twin aims: to improve housing by clearing slums, and to end the prostitution which was endemic around Cable Street in the 1950s. He had a media profile as 'The Prostitute's Padre' and was popular locally, but his approach tied improved social conditions to the demolition of Georgian terraces. "Bulldozers", he said, "are the only way to clear Stepney of its shocking vice". A 1961 *Daily Mail* article, headlined 'Miracle in Stepney', includes a remarkable photograph of Father Joe on his knees in the street giving thanks as the houses of the now-vanished Sander Street are pulled down. "I have never seen anything so ruddy rotten as the square mile I have got here in my parish", he said.[18] Father Joe left in 1962, by which time the final decision had been taken to dismantle Wellclose.

The two squares were replaced during the 1970s by the St. George's Estate, a mix of low, medium and high rise blocks. The new buildings reconfigured the street pattern, eliminating the basic shapes of the two squares. Three towers occupy what was the north side of Swedenborg Square and the highest, Shearsmith House, is among the tallest buildings in Britain. However, redevelopment plans were never fully implemented and by the time St. George's Estate was complete it was already out-of-date.

The redevelopment visited on Wellclose, for all its good intentions, created a place that is dislocated, dominated by traffic and very difficult to navigate, either geographically or conceptually. It has become scattered and its many parts hidden or, like Swedenborg's skull, lost in the depths of history. An act of faith is needed to resurrect the spirit of the old Wellclose.

REFERENCES

1   Coverley, Merlin, *Occult London*, Pocket Essentials, 2008

2   Nairn, Ian, *Nairn's London*, Penguin 1966

3   Glinert, Ed, *East End Chronicles*, Penguin 2003

4   Sinclair, Iain, *London Orbital*, Penguin 2002

5   Defoe, Daniel, *A Tour Through the Whole Island of Great Britain*, Penguin 1978

6   'Swedish Lutheran Church, Prince's Square (1729-1911)'
      http://www.stgite.org.uk undated, uncredited, accessed 5th March 2014

7   Dickens, Charles, 'Last of Old Stories Retold: The Accident at the Brunswick
      Theatre' *All the Year Round. Volume XX.* 13 June – 28 November, 1868

8   'History of the Parish, St.George-in-the-East' stgite.org.uk (undated, uncredited
      accessed October 2012)

9   Greenwood, James, *The Wilds of London*, Guildford 1874

10   McKie, Jean, "Alphons Elder, Street Musician", 2009
      www.jeaned.net/AlphonsEderBookrevised2009.pdf

11   Greenwood, James, "Mysteries of Modern London", 1882

12   *ibid*

13   *ibid*

14   Wilde, Oscar, *The Picture of Dorian Gray*, Wordsworth Classics 1992

15   Zangwill, Israel, *Ghetto Comedies*, Heinemann 1907

16   Booth, Charles, *Survey Into Life and Labour in London 1886-1903*, LSE Charles
      Booth Online Archive

17   Nairn, Ian, *Nairn's London*, Penguin 1966

18   *History of the Parish, St.George-in-the-East*. stgite.org.uk (undated, uncredited
      accessed 5th March 2013)

WHITE CITY: THE FIRST OLYMPIC PARK

*This patch of flat land north of Shepherd's Bush
hides a very different identity as a place with
a spectacular past – gleaming white pavilions,
pleasure palaces, fantastical fairground rides
and entertainment on a scale never before seen.*

Introduction

White City is best known as a stop on the Central Line with the BBC and an estate attached, not as a tourist attraction. However, this patch of flat land north of Shepherd's Bush hides a very different identity as a place with a spectacular past – gleaming white pavilions, pleasure palaces, fantastical fairground rides and entertainment on a scale never before seen. Low grade scrubland, then on the edge of London, was redeveloped at great expense for a London Olympics, complete with new stadium, new stations and a new park – London's first Olympic Park. It was a roaring success, the best entertainment Edwardian London had to offer, and the favourite day out for a pre-

First World War generation. Yet the attraction of its day was, within 30 years, dilapidated and well on the way to obscurity and demolition.

White City today is little visited except by those who live in the self-contained White City Estate, or frequent the BBC enclave on its edge. Its past life is largely forgotten and White City is hemmed in by urban motorways. However, the aura of the 1908 Olympics and the great Franco-British exhibition can still be detected among the acres of London County Council blocks, the Westway traffic, and the dead screens of the abandoned BBC Television Centre.

The Wormwood

Shepherd's Bush was a village on the long road leading west out of London, separated from the city until new railway lines reeled it into London's orbit in the mid-19th century. In the 1840s, despite the West London Railway running through the area, Shepherd's Bush was still a tiny place mostly notable for the ponds that surrounded it on all sides.

Syndercombe Cottage was a characteristic building, a long low thatched house on the corner of Goldhawk Road and Shepherd's Bush Green. It proved a discreet rural hideaway for its owner, Miles Syndercombe, who cooked up a plot there in 1657 to assassinate the Lord Protector, Oliver Cromwell. Syndercombe, a former Parliamentary soldier, built an ambitious new weapon – an improvised cannon made by tying seven blunderbusses together – with which he planned to ambush Cromwell as he rode to Hampton Court. It failed to work and Syndercombe was betrayed before he could put his back-up plan into action, which involved setting fire to Whitehall Palace. He was arrested and condemned to death, but persuaded his sister to smuggle poison into his Tower of London cell where he committed suicide. His naked body was staked to the ground on Tower Hill, and left there to discourage further conspiracies. His cottage, however, survived well beyond its era and was only demolished in 1891.

Beyond Shepherd's Bush to the north-west was Wormholt Wood, which perhaps means the 'snake-infested wood', and Wormwood Scrubs – an obscure area of wasteland with poor soil, used for grazing and cutting firewood. Wormwood Scrubs Prison opened on the Scrubs in 1874, in what was then rural isolation. As far back as 1812, part of Wormwood Scrubs was leased to the Government for use as a military training ground, and the War Office retained an interest in what was usefully flat, low value land not far from Central London. The training ground was used by the War Office until the end of the 19th century, and hangars for docking airships were built on the Scrubs at the start of the 1900s, later used to house Navy blimps during the First World War. The land were still being used by the military in 1940 when the world's entire supply of heavy water, essential to producing the nuclear bomb, was smuggled out of France ahead of the German invasion and stored at Wormwood Scrubs, before being moved to the ultimate safe house at Windsor Castle.

As well as the military, there were also tiny indications of what was to come. In 1894 Wood House, an early 19th century house on the east side of Wood Lane, opened as a public pleasure ground called Woodhouse Park. The building, its gardens shaded by vast cedars, looked like several houses of different shapes and sizes squeezed together. The Wood Lane railway depot was later built on the site.

The Hammersmith and City Railway, which opened in 1864, tied Shepherd's Bush umbilically to the City of London with a direct link to Farringdon, and made its future as a convenient suburb inevitable. The Central Line, the first deep-level tube in London, brought even faster commuting in 1900 and the first electric trams ran to the City in 1901. Shepherd's Bush Market arrived in 1914.

Change was, however, gradual and a photo of 1908 shows hay fields with the turreted roofline of Wormwood Scrubs prison silhouetted against the horizon. In 1908, beyond the new Edwardian terraced streets north of the Uxbridge Road, was Old Oak Farm, the farmhouse sited near what is now the junction between Bloemfontein Road and Australia Road.

But in 1908 a very different future was on the horizon for Old Oak Farm. Attention had turned to this obscure part of town, and a site described as "desolate-looking fields… which looked as though they were tired of being country but not quite ready to be town."[1] It was the ideal location for a hugely ambitious building project which would shortly become the talk of the town. On edgelands next door to Edwardian suburbs, the White City would be born.

A new type of exhibition

Large 'exhibitions', featuring displays of goods and spectacular entertainments, became popular across Europe during the 1860s and 1870s. They reached West London in 1887 when an entrepreneur called John Robinson Whitley led the development of land near the railway at Earl's Court, where he staged a show called The American Exhibition. This featured 'Buffalo Bill' Cody's Wild West Show and was a sensation, attracting William Gladstone and the Prince of Wales to see Buffalo Bill's cowboys and Sioux warriors. This success was followed by a series of annual shows including Italian (with a 'Rome under the Caesars' amphitheatre); French (a 'Wild East' show, with French Africans); and German (German castles were blown up every afternoon and evening, annoying the local residents). Then Imre Kiralfy arrived on the scene, a Hungarian-born showman who had made his name in the United States. Kiralfy had worked with P.T. Barnum on 'America: a Grand Historical Spectacle' at the Chicago World's Fair of 1893. Kiralfy presided at Earl's Court from 1895 until 1903, putting on a series of populist Imperial spectaculars including 'Our Naval Victories' and 'China – the Relief of the Legations'. This was all just a preparation for his ultimate project, the new exhibition at White City.

The original idea came from the French Chamber of Commerce

in London, to celebrate the Entente Cordiale of 1904 with a display of industrial achievements. The concept was developed to include Britain, France and their Imperial possessions, on a scale never seen before in Britain.

Imre Kiralfy was employed to oversee the design of the entire exhibition, working as a family team with his two brothers Albert and Charles. Building was co-supervised by English and French architects, Marius Toudoire and John Belcher, with 13 others employed to work on the many pavilions.

Old Oak Farm itself was demolished for the exhibition site and Bloemfontein Road extended north into 140 acres of semi-rural wasteland, an area eight times the size of the Great Exhibition in 1851. The main pavilions were built west of Wood Lane, but the exhibition stretched all the way from what is now Shepherd's Bush Central Line station to the Westway.

To the east of Wood Lane 'The Tall Buildings' were constructed on plots leased from the railway companies. These were halls connecting the tube station to the main exhibition built on steel stilts, 30 feet off the ground, over the live railway lines running underneath. The Tall Buildings were packed tightly into limited space, in some places only three feet away from houses. The Westfield Shopping Centre, which now occupies the site, recreates the effect by looming large behind Caxton Road and the surrounding terraces.

The exhibition buildings were built by 4,000 men working during the day and 2,000 by night. They constructed a fantasia of pristine white stucco pavilions, which immediately became known as 'The White City'. There were 20 'palaces', one 120 pavilions, half a mile of waterways, ornamental gardens, lagoons, bridges, tree-lined avenues. The buildings cheerfully combined Arabian, Rococo and Tudor styles to unique, indescribable effect. The main entrance on Wood Lane was a flamboyant, wedding cake pavilion, looking like a fairground railway terminus. Despite their carnival aesthetics, the buildings were substantial and the site looked like a mirage of a city, beamed from a far-away desert.

Butter mountain

The Franco-British Exhibition was opened by King Edward VII and President Fallières of France on 26th May 1908, and ran for only five months, closing on 31st October 1908. By this time the brilliant white buildings had started to look a little grubby.

Arriving at Shepherd's Bush station, one hundred thousand visitors a day processed through the Exhibition Halls on their stilts, where a combination of displays showed British and French industry and arts. These were organised by the London County Council, and their rather stern approach contrasted with the entertainment laid on by the Kiralfys at the main site. The 14 halls added up to a long walk, something that proved a problem for later exhibitions on the site. They included the British Social Economy Hall (an odd selection of sporting rifles and rods, information on road-building in the City of Westminster, and samples of Harrogate spa water); the French Liberal Arts Section (a not particularly liberal or artistic selection of books, prints, chemical products, leather, sporting goods); the French Textile Section (fancy French finery) and the Section of Woman's Work (including the original manuscript of *Jane Eyre* and Florence Nightingale's carriage).

The pavilions on the main site were more flamboyant than the Exhibition Halls, and more entertaining. They combined an eclectic and somewhat bizarre selection of themes and exhibits. French and British colonies had their own pavilions, and the Canadian Pavilion featured a grand display of 'sculptured butter', a three-dimensional representation of the meeting between explorer Jacques Cartier and Donnacona in 1535 (important Canadian history, no doubt), as well as a buttery Edward VII, all inside a large refrigerated glass cabinet.

Most of the entertainment, however, took place outside, where the real attractions were to be found. The centrepiece of the showground was the Court of Honour, a pavilion with illuminated fountains and a lake for swan boat rides. In the Indian Arena, a vast white building staged acrobats, sorcerers, tightrope-walkers, wrestlers, snake-charmers; races between men and animals; a 50-animal procession; and a herd of working elephants, 12 of which careered down a slide into the lake below as a finale.

A life-size Irish Village was set up in one corner of the site, with a stone Celtic cross, a timber framed hall, white-washed thatched cottages, and a tall Rapunzel-style stone tower with a pointed roof. The authentic atmosphere was completed by girls in peasant costumes riding donkeys. Nor was the Irish Village the only ethnographic fun on offer. There was a Ceylon Village, with dancers, jugglers, musicians and elephants that visitors could ride on, and a Senegalese Village for which 150 Senegalese spent five months living in mud huts in Shepherd's Bush. Rickshaw drivers were also brought over from Asia to drive visitors around.

Flip-Flap

There was also a major fairground element to the entertainment, which proved the most popular aspect of the exhibition. A total of 2.8 million people rode on the Scenic Railway, which had one mile of track passing through a medley of scenery from different continents including mountains, valleys, lakes, waterfalls and illuminated tunnels, all at 50 miles per hour.

The 'Flip-Flap' became the symbol of the whole exhibition, a terrifying-looking fairground ride (6d a time) which would not look at all out of place in a modern amusement park. Two long, wooden arms swung carriages 200 feet into the air in opposite directions, flying past each other on the way. It even inspired a popular song called 'Take me on the Flip-Flap': "Good old London's in a maze / with its very latest craze / and every day in crowds we fight and push / on

Dorando Close, White City

a motor-bus to climb / twenty-seven at a time / or take a good old Tube to Shepherd's Bush" etc. etc. There were other rides too: the Spiral, which gently corkscrewed to the top before plummeting like a stone; and the Mountain Slide which recreated the experience of downhill skiing.

The Kiralfy style was evident in the multi-media extravaganzas, some of which were in dubious taste such as a spectacular electrical and mechanical recreation of the 1889 Johnstown Flood that had killed 5,000 people, and set-piece firework displays representing car and rail crashes. There was the first demonstration of the Stereomatos, an entirely new system a century ahead of its time, which projected 3D colour images onto a screen.

The 1908 Exhibition closed with firework displays involving Britannia and Marianne, and St. George slaying a dragon. Amid the celebrations, a group of a hundred young men wearing Votes for Women badges caused trouble in the crowd, letting off their own fireworks.

The range of attractions, exhibitions and entertainments was a fascinating combination of the strange, the colonial and the genuinely impressive, all in the improbable setting of W12. An aerial view of White City shows the huge sweep of the banked stadium seating, a Canadian Toboggan rollercoaster, a Lyons' Tea Room, native huts and the huge Scenic Railway – a monorail ride carved through the side of a gigantic, plaster mountain, looming over neat terraced rows of houses, with the Kensal Green gasholders in the distance.

The first London Olympics

Remarkably, the Franco-British Exhibition was not the only major event on the White City site during the summer of 1908. Time and space were also found to stage the Olympics. The modern Olympics were still in development, having been relaunched in Athens in 1896 by Baron de Coubertin. Subsequent Olympiads were staged as side-shows at the Paris Exposition in 1900 and the World's Fair at St. Louis in 1904. The fourth Games was scheduled for Rome in 1908, but the Italian Prime Minister was not enthusiastic and used the 1906 eruption of Mount Vesuvius as an excuse to withdraw. An offer was made to stage the Games in London instead, and the Franco-British exhibition organisers agreed to pay for the construction of a new stadium in exchange for 75 per cent of the gate receipts.

The 1908 Games were organised by the Management Committee of the Olympic Games, who set themselves up in the new Imperial Sports Club in the centre of the exhibition site, conveniently next door to the Moët and Chandon pavilion. The White City Stadium was purpose-built to stage track and field events and proved the most lasting feature of the site, remaining in use until the 1980s.

The Games lasted from April to October, longer even than the

Franco-British Exhibition and in fact so long that many competitors
had to go home, giving the home nations a very useful advantage.
This was one of a number of aspects of the organisation which
meant that this was the last time a host country was allowed to take
charge. The final British medal haul of 145 is unlikely to be surpassed,
partly because Britain can no longer supply all the officials. Nor,
disappointingly, can it include sports that only it practises, such
as small-bore shooting, while leaving out sports at which it is not
very good.

Matters came to a head in the 400 metres, which was re-run on the
orders of the officials after the British favourite was allegedly pushed
off the track. All the other competitors refused to take part and the
British runner Wyndham Halswelle, the only competitor, won gold in
splendid isolation. However, the 1908 Olympics are best remembered
for the marathon. Before 1921 there was no set distance for the race,
and the 1908 race was run from Windsor Castle to the White City
Stadium, a distance of 26 miles 385 yards. The extra 385 yards were
added because Queen Alexandria asked for the race to finish in front
of the Royal Box, and this later became the standard distance.

The marathon is famous for the performance of Dorando Pietri, a
22-year-old, moustachioed Italian runner. He supposedly discovered
his endurance talents in 1904, while training as a pastry chef in Carpi,
near Modena. He spotted a race on the way home from work and
took part still wearing his work clothes, beating Pericle Pagliani, the
top Italian runner of his time. Coming to London he was in scorching
form, but he pushed the pace too hard. He entered the stadium in the
lead, but collapsed five times on the way to the finishing line, helped
to his feet by race umpires.

A very well-known photograph shows him in huge, black shorts
and head-kerchief, knees buckling as he breasts the tape, Edwardian
gentlemen rushing to support him. The vista behind the small crowd
reveals grass and trees as far as the eye can see.

Pietri was disqualified for receiving help to finish the race, triggering fights in the stands, but his determination to finish made him famous. Irving Berlin wrote a song called 'Dorando' about him; he competed in exhibition races in the States, and Sir Arthur Conan Doyle led a public subscription to help him open a bakery back home. He is commemorated by Dorando Close, on the edge of the White City Estate.

The world in White City

The success of the Franco-British exhibition led the Kiralfys to set White City up as a permanent, annual exhibition venue. In 1909 they staged the International Imperial Exhibition, on the same lines but with more countries, a new Imperial Pavilion and a Scottish Village, with piping, tweed-making and its own post office to go with the Irish Village from the previous year which was brought back, possibly by popular demand.

The Japan-British Exhibition followed in 1910, with Japanese pagodas, tea-houses and gardens against a painted mountain backdrop, with wrestlers, and an aging 'bear-killer'. There was, of course, a village – this time with Ainu minority people living in reed huts. There was also a Japanese Garden, expanded from the 1908 Exhibition, a remodelled version of which exists in Hammersmith Park as the only intact survival from the Exhibition site. The Coronation Exhibition of 1911 showed models of the Taj Mahal, the Pagan Temple of Burma, and the Golden Monastery of Mandalay. There was also a display of bird boxes.

In 1912 the Latin-British exhibition was themed, rather widely, around the Latin people of France, Italy, Portugal and Spain. The Flip-Flap was rebuilt so its carriages revolved, and buildings were remodelled. Electric trams were introduced to carry visitors around, and there was a 'Life-Saving at Sea' exhibition. By this time, the exhibition themes were becoming a little half-hearted, and in 1913

Japanese Garden, Hammersmith Park

the National Gas Exhibition and Congress – all about gas – suggested
that the years of spectacle at White City were past. The final show at
White City was the Anglo-American exhibition of 1914. It involved
huge models of the Panama Canal, New York and the Grand Canyon
and a Wild West show, harking back to Kiralfy's earliest triumphs.
When war broke out in August it closed and was taken over by the
Army for basic and medical training. This gave new conscripts an
unrivalled opportunity to mess around on the rides and exhibits, some
of which had to be dismantled when soldiers were injured.

Between the wars

After the war the Army handed part of the site back to Charles Kiralfy
in 1920 (Imre had died in 1919) but the Government occupied the
Tall Buildings and the stadium. The Exhibition Company decided to

sell the exhibition site in 1922 because it was costing too much to maintain. The buyer, the Holborn Empire Company, pulled out at the last minute leaving the whole place empty for several years. Charles Kiralfy wrote to the Times in 1924 suggesting it should be used for the Imperial War Museum.

The Tall Buildings, however, were reclaimed from the Government and used every year between 1921 and 1929 for the British Industries Fair, then for textile fairs until 1937. They suffered from competition for trade fairs from the more modern facilities at Earl's Court and Olympia. The British Industries Fair moved to Olympia after complaints that people had to walk too far to get in at White City, and that the halls were draughty. The final straw appears to have been a dense fog that covered Shepherd's Bush during all ten days of the final show, in February 1929.

The exhibition site was, by this time, no longer looking its best and had been left for the most part to decay – "the rotten ribs of the White City",[2] as it was described in a novel of the time. An amusement park called Playlands had opened opposite the entrance on Wood Lane in 1934, with a 'Looping the Loop' rollercoaster and a miniature version of the Brooklands racetrack, but did not last long.

Station to station

Shepherd's Bush is one of the most connected parts of London, and also one of the most confusing, possessing five separate underground stations within a ten-minute walk: Shepherd's Bush, Wood Lane, White City, Shepherd's Bush Market and Goldhawk Road. The White City exhibition site is to blame, and untangling the sequence of events is a particular challenge.

The first Wood Lane underground station, the western terminus of the Central Line, was specially built for the Franco-British Exhibition in 1908. It had a loop to send trains back the other way, but when the Central Line was extended beyond Shepherd's Bush this proved a

Westway, White City

problem and it was replaced by a new White City station in 1947. The old platforms could be seen from passing trains until the 2000s, when they were cleared for the Westfield development.

However, there was a second Wood Lane station nearby, also built especially for the exhibition, on the Metropolitan Railway (now the Hammersmith & City Line). It was unhelpfully renamed Wood Lane (White City) in 1920 and then White City in 1947, and closed in 1959 following a fire. Until 2008, when the current Wood Lane station opened on the Hammersmith & City Line, there was no Wood Lane station – just the bricked up façade of the old Metropolitan Railway station. To round matters off, until 2008 there were also two Shepherd's Bush stations, one on the Central Line and the other on the Hammersmith & City Line. The latter was renamed Shepherd's Bush Market in a belated attempt to make its location a little clearer, despite being in fact very convenient for Wood Lane. The multiple routes to Shepherd's Bush and White City are a legacy from the years when all of London wanted to be here.

Gone to the dogs

The White City Stadium, which had been built for the Olympics, was the lasting legacy of the exhibition site. It was the first purpose-built stadium for an Olympic Games, with seats for 68,000 people although its capacity was considerably higher. It was built as a temporary structure, but became a fixture. It was used for athletics until 1914 and was then converted to a greyhound track in 1926, which is the way most Londoners remember it. It was also used by Queen's Park Rangers Football Club for two years from 1931, and for a year by the White City Rebels speedway team. Baseball was briefly popular in Britain in the 1930s, and a White City team played in the London Major Baseball League. Athletics came back to the stadium in the 1930s, with AAA meetings held there.

In 1939 82,000 people watched a boxing match between Len Harvey and Jock McAvoy. The height of the stadium's fame was also the peak of greyhound racing's huge popularity before the Second World War, when it was known as 'the governor' of tracks. Mick the Miller, the only greyhound with name recognition, won the Greyhound Derby there in 1929 and 1930 and headlines in the newspapers read "100,000 Pack White City."

Robert Westerby's 1937 novel *Wide Boys Never Work* conjures up the heyday of the White City dog track. Wide boy Jim Bankley, part of a criminal gang working Soho and White City, talks about "…this maze of walks, this huge structure of steel and concrete, and glass, the polite attendants, the carpeted stairs and diffused lighting–Caw ! It was an eye-opener."[3]

Westerby describes "Bookies and their women, impermanently jewelled; a few people in evening-dress; a crowd of youngsters in good clothes; all sorts, all with one idea. The management provided the setting, the comfort, the luxury, the sport. Society, or civilisation, or what-you-will provided the rest. Two thousand Mugs to every Wide Boy: professional gamblers, basking in temporary opulence; hangers-on and rabbit-faced tipsters, noses sniffing after the dirty stink of dirty money."[4]

White City played a role in the 1966 World Cup, hosting a match between France and Uruguay because, oddly enough, Wembley was booked for greyhound racing and unavailable. Dog racing continued until 1983, when its declining popularity persuaded the owners to sell up. The Pogues wrote a bleak song about its decline, 'White City': "Oh the torn up ticket stubs / From a hundred thousand mugs / Now washed away with dead dreams in the rain / And the car-parks going up / And they're pulling down the pubs / And it's just another bloody rainy day."[5]

The stadium was demolished in 1984, and became the site of a new BBC development called Media Village (not to be confused with an actual village or a Scottish or Senegalese version). The stadium finishing line is marked on the site, and a list of 1908 medal-winners is on the wall beside the entrance.

White City Estate

In 1938 the London County Council bought most of the exhibition land to the west side of Wood Lane, and began to clear the once-white dream palaces for housing. They laid out an entirely new street grid with road names referring back to the colonial themes of the exhibitions – Australia Road, South Africa Road, Canada Way, India Way. The LCC's unmistakable blocks were springing up all over London but the White City Estate was one of the largest new developments of the time, a complete district consisting entirely of five-storey, red-brick blocks.

The Blue Lamp, a sharp-edged Ealing film that spawned the soft-centred *Dixon of Dock Green* television series, revolves around post-war White City. PC George Dixon is based at Paddington Green Police Station and the film occupies the area between the Edgware Road and White City. It culminates in a car chase through Shepherd's Bush, a foot chase along Wood Lane and a final, violent showdown among the crowds watching the greyhounds at the White City Stadium. The shabby, bomb-damaged streets conceal a typically inner London collision of classes, much as they do now: "It ain't so fresh round here. But I like it. Funny district this, you know. Neither fish nor fowl nor good red herring. Some rotten slums, filthy – and some luxury flats. Middle class and working class and all sort lumped together sometimes in one road. Queer."[6]

The White City Estate developed a reputation as the frontline of West London, separated from upwardly mobile Notting Hill by a motorway, with the BBC stranded on the wrong side. As White City novelist Courttia Newland put it "Who could've planned putting a multi-million pound government-funded industry bang next door to a funding-starved council estate. Madmen maybe? It was crazy, but that was the way London was built and it had been that way for centuries."[7] In the mid-80s Pete Townshend released a concept album called *White City: The Novel* which portrays the Estate as the kind of place where a version of Jimmy, the doomed hero of *Quadrophenia*, ends up trapped while his dreams run into the sand. The accompanying *White City: The Film* features evocative footage of dole queues and skinheads kicking cans outside the South Africa Fish Bar.

The BBC at White City

If White City has any 21st century public profile it belongs to the BBC, which first moved there in the late 1950s. The Corporation had bought part of the derelict exhibition site in 1947, and began work on a new Television Centre in 1950, but post-war restrictions on building materials meant that it did not open until 1960. The building with its brick façade, 'atomic dots', and central glass doughnut became famous, associated with countless national events and television highlights. It was used to shoot most of the BBC's television output, from *Doctor Who* and *Monty Python* to *Blue Peter* and *Fawlty Towers*. Its closure in 2013 put a definitive end to the analogue broadcasting era.

While the BBC waited for Television Centre to be completed in the 1950s, it occupied the former Gaumont Studios, in Lime Grove, just to the south of White City. They had opened in 1915, next door to a home for fallen women called Urania Cottage, which was run by Charles Dickens and the benefactor Angela Burdett-Coutts. Gaumont-British rebuilt the studios in 1932 as the best equipped of their era, a fine whitewashed modernist block with an embossed brick 'G' on the façade. Lime Grove was used to film a sizeable portion of British cinema's pre-war output, with over 700 Gaumont and Gainsborough pictures made there – films such as *Fanny by Gaslight*, *Man of Aran*, *Waterloo Road*, and *The Wicked Lady,* and early Hitchcock films including *The 39 Steps*. The BBC moved there in 1949 as a temporary measure but carried on using the studios until 1991, by which time they were in a poor state and referred to by staff as 'Slime Grove'. The building was demolished in 1993.

Decay and unrest

By the 1980s, the former Tall Buildings site between Wood Lane and Uxbridge Road was forgotten and derelict. The empty halls, three times the height of the adjacent houses, loomed over the surrounding streets. The film-set entrance arch remained standing, painted green and converted along with the first two halls into offices for Arrow Life Insurance. The halls had been used as hangars and as construction space for gliders and parachutes during the Second World War. Later the City Display Organisation used them to build film and television sets. One of the halls was leased by the Vanderbilt Racquet Club during the 1970s.

White City Underground Station

The whole area was in a long-term limbo, traffic endlessly crawling past unwanted development opportunities, heading somewhere else. The West Cross Route, the short stretch of urban motorway separating Shepherd's Bush from Notting Hill, became the symbolic centre of the 1990s anti-roads protest movement. Reclaim the Streets, an anti-car direct action group, held illegal street parties in 1995 on Camden High Street and Upper Street in Islington. On 13th July 1996 they closed the M41 to White City, set up a sound system and drilled holes in the road surface beneath the skirts of giant Marie Antoinette dolls, before planting trees in the tarmac.

Nicholas Royle's novel *The Director's Cut* is set partly among the derelict exhibition halls of the 1990s, the central character Munro drawn to the area as "the only address he knew in London, from watching so much television as a child."[8] Munro ends up living in the

abandoned Wood Lane tube station, still equipped with a sign reading:
"WOOD LANE
ALIGHT FOR
EXHIBITION"

The halls had by this time lost their sheen: "The floor was a sticky
carpet of asbestos dust, pigeon droppings and white feathers. The
skeletal remains of a series of tiny rooms lined the east wall. Rusty
steps leading up to an unsteady-looking balcony were missing several
treads. Long, narrow light fittings hung at crazy angles from the
ceiling like the broken wings of huge birds; their fluorescent tubes lay
in a million pieces on the floor, time having worn their edges as soft as
the feathers with which they mingled."[9]

In London few large sites lie empty for long without acquiring a
series of unbuilt or unbuildable projects. During the 1970s there were
plans to use the Tall Buildings site for a new railway goods depot, as
part of an abortive attempt to build a Channel Tunnel. The London
Borough of Hammersmith and Fulham later wanted the site for
housing. By the time *The Director's Cut* was published in 2000, time
had finally been called on the Tall Buildings. They were demolished
in 2003-04 in preparation for the eventual building of the Westfield
Shopping Centre. The entrance arch came down in July 2003.

Future city

The western half of the White City site is now under the pseudo-
streets of Westfield, an updated version of the fantasy land created on
the site a century before. Westfield squats opposite the White City
estate, over the buses and cars of Wood Lane. The only real physical
remnant of the exhibition is Hammersmith Park (which is confusingly
not in Hammersmith at all), remodelled on the site of the original
exhibition park and containing the Japanese Garden.

The White City estate is oddly cut-off, an island around which the rest of London circles without ever dropping in. It still has the feel of the edge-of-town site it was when the Kiralfys arrived, although London has since grown far beyond it. The proximity of the BBC emphasises the division between global focus and obscurity, with a procession of taxis on Wood Lane taking presenters and executives back to very different parts of town. Ed Glinert dismisses White City as "a 50-acre council estate of unrelenting dreariness".[10] However, as the inner London council estate becomes an endangered species, appreciation is likely to grow for a neighbourhood of well-constructed, unfussy LCC blocks, the like of which will not be built again.

Eyes are turning to White City as the boundary of central London bulges west, with much-delayed plans to rebuild Queen's Park Rangers' ground at Loftus Road, and a new Imperial College campus coming to the site north of Westfield. For now though, White City remains hidden in plain sight, on the tube map but off the radar, still recovering from a century long, post-exhibition hangover.

REFERENCES

1   Journal of the Society of Arts, referenced in Kimber, Jane and Wheeldon, Anne, *Images of London: Shepherd's Bush and White City*, Tempus 2005

2   Bowen, Elizabeth, *To The North*, Penguin 1945

3   Westerby, Robert, *Wide Boys Never Work*, John Lehmann 1937

4   *ibid*

5   The Pogues, 'White City', *Peace and Love*, Island 1989

6   Willis, Ted, *The Blue Lamp*, Convoy Publications Ltd. 1950

7   Newland, Courttia, *The Scholar*, Abacus 2001

8   Royle, Nicholas, *The Director's Cut*, Abacus 2000

9   *ibid*

10   Glinert, Ed, *The London Compendium*, Penguin 2004

BIBLIOGRAPHY

GENERAL

Booth, Charles (1886-1903), *Survey Into Life and Labour in London 1886-1903*, LSE Charles Booth Online Archive

Davies, Philip (2011), *Lost London 1870-1945*, Transatlantic Press

Saunders, Ann (ed.) (2005) *The London County Council Bomb Damage Maps 1939-45*, London Topographical Society

1. CLARE MARKET & OLD DRURY LANE: THE LOST ROOKERY

Allen, Thomas (1837) *The history and antiquities of London, Westminster, Southwark, and parts adjacent*, Cowie and Strange

Andrew, Donna T. (ed.) (1994) *London Debating Societies 1776-1799*, London Record Society

Anon. (1728), *A View of London and Westminster: or, The Town Spy*, T. Warner

Aumonier, Stacy (1922) 'Where Was Wych Street?', in O'Brien, Edward J. & Cournos, John, (ed.) *The Best British Short Stories of 1922*, Periodical Publications, Boston

Beames, Thomas (1852) *The Rookeries of London*, Thomas Bosworth

Cooke, William (1804) *Memoirs of Charles Macklin, Comedian*, James Asperne

Cunningham, Peter (1849) *A Handbook for London Past and Present*, John Murray

Dickens, Charles (the Younger) (1888) *Dickens' Dictionary of London*

www.victorianlondon.org/publications/dictionary.htm

Diprose, John (1876) *Some account of the parish of St Clement Danes*, Diprose and Bateman

Fenn, Colin (2010) 'The Cost of Burial at Norwood', *Friends of West Norwood Cemetery Newsletter*, No.68, May 2010

Gay, John (2003) *Selected Poems*, Fyfield Books

Gissing, George (1993) *New Grub Street*, Oxford University Press

Goldsmith, Oliver (1997) *Everyman Poetry Library No. 30*, J.M. Dent

Gordon, Charles (1903) *Old Time Aldwych The Kingsway and Neighbourhood*, T. Fisher Unwin

Hobley, Brian (1988) 'Saxon London: *Lundenwic* and *Lundenburg*: two cities rediscovered', in Hodges, Richard and Hobley, Brian, *The Rebirth of Towns in the West AD 700-1050*, CBA Research Report No.68, Council for British Archaeology

Howell, James (1657) *Londinopolis: an historical discourse*, Twiford

Hubert D. & Sutcliffe, J. (1996) 'The 'Haussmannization' of London?: The Planning and Construction of Kingsway-Aldwych 1889-1935', *Planning Perspectives*, Vol. 11, No.2, April 1996, E&FN Spon

Kiloh, George (2008) *A History of LSE's Buildings*, London School of Economics

Kiloh, George, *LSE Complete*, unpublished manuscript

Pepys, Samuel (1660) *The Diary of Samuel Pepys* Vol. 1. University of California Press 2000

Pepys, Samuel (1664) *The Diary of Samuel Pepys* Vol. 5. University of California Press 2000

Pepys, Samuel (1667) *The Diary of Samuel Pepys* Vol. 8. University of California Press 2000

Pope, Alexander (1989) *Collected Poems*, J.M. Dent

Ritchie, J. Ewing (1880) *Days and Nights in London*, Tinsley Bros.

Rogers, Pat (2005) The Maypole in the Strand: Pope and the Politics of Revelry', *Journal for Eighteenth-Century Studies*, Vol. 28, Issue 1, March 2005

Secara, Margaret Pierce (ed.) (1999) *The Arraignment, Tryal, and Condemnation of Robert Earl of Essex*, Thos. Basset, Sam. Heyrick, and Matth. Gillyflower, 1679 www.elizabethan.org/trial/index.html

Shakespeare, William (1600) *Henry IV Part 2*, Arden Shakespeare 1967

Strype, John (1720) *A Survey of the Cities of London and Westminster*

Thornbury, Walter (1878) *Old and New London: Volume 1*, Cassell

Thornbury, Walter (1879) *Old and New London: Volume 3*, Cassell

Trusler, Rev. Dr. John (1786) The London Adviser and Guide, Printed for the author

Wheatley, Henry Benjamin, and Cunningham, Peter (1891) *London Past and Present*, Cambridge University Press 2011

Wood, Mrs Henry (1869) *Roland Yorke*, Richard Bentley

2. CRIPPLEGATE: THE FIERY CITY

Baddeley, Sir John (1922) *Cripplegate: one of the twenty-six wards of the City of London,* Hodder & Stoughton

Black, Jeremy (2009) *London,* Carnegie Publishing

Blyth, Harry (1894) 'The Accusing Shadow' in Cox, M. (ed.) (2003) *The Oxford Book of Victorian Detective Stories*, Oxford University Press

Cross, Nigel (1985) *The Common Writer: Life in Nineteenth Century Grub Street*, Cambridge University Press

Denton, W. (1883) *Records of St Giles' Cripplegate*, George Bell & Sons

Dickens, Charles (1844) *Martin Chuzzlewit*, Penguin 2000

Gissing, George, *New Grub Street*, Oxford University Press 1993

Halleck, Reuben Post (1913) *Halleck's New English Literature*, American Book Company

Hibbert, C. (1980, first published 1969) *London, The Biography of a City*, Penguin

Inwood, S. (1998) *A History of London*, Macmillan

Macaulay, Rose (1958) *The World My Wilderness*, Penguin

Nicholl, Charles (2007) *The Lodger: Shakespeare on Silver Street*, WF Howes Ltd.

Noorthouck, John, (1773) *A New History of London, Including Westminster and Southwark*, R. Baldwin

Paton Walsh, Jill (1972) *Fireweed*, Puffin

Rogers, Pat (1972) *Hacks and Dunces: Pope, Swift and Grub Street*, University Paperbacks

Sinclair, Iain (1997) *Lights Out for the Territory*, Granta

Strype, John (1720) *A Survey of the Cities of London and Westminster*

Thornbury, Walter (1879) *Old and New London: Volume 2*, Cassell

Trench, Richard (1989) *London Before the Blitz*, Weidenfeld & Nicolson

Turner, E.S. (1998) *Unholy Pursuits: The Wayward Parsons of Grub Street*, The Book Guild Ltd.

Maitland, William (1775) *The history of London from its foundation to the present time ... including the several parishes in Westminster, Middlesex, Southwark, &c., within the bills of mortality*, J. Wilkie

3. HORSELEYDOWN, ST. OLAVE AND PICKLE HERRING

Barnes, Gordon L. (1980) *The District of St Mark's Bermondsey*, self-published, in Southwark Local Archives

Barnett, Richard (2013) 'This Parliament of Monsters: London's spectacular fairs', sickcityproject.wordpress.com accessed 18th December 2013

Besant, Walter (1912) *London South of the Thames*, Adam & Charles Black 1912

Corner, G.R. (1855) *The History of Horselydown*, Surrey Archaeological Society Paper, 30th October 1855

Chaucer, Geoffrey (1475) *The Canterbury Tales*, Oxford World's Classics 2008

Doré, Gustave and Jerrold Blanchard, (1872) *London: A Pilgrimage*, Grant & Co.

Moore, Alan and Campbell, Eddie (2006) *From Hell*, Knockabout

Moss, Arthur B. 'Waterside London' in G.R. Sims (ed.) (1902) *Living London: Its Work and Its Play, Its Humour and Its Pathos, Its Sights and Its Scenes*, Vol. 2 Cassell and Company

Orwell, George, *Down and Out In Paris and London*, Penguin 1933

Pepys, Samuel (1666) *The Diary of Samuel Pepys* Vol. 7. University of California Press 1995

Rendle, William & Norman, Philip (1888) *The Inns of Old Southwark and their Associations*, Longmans, Green & Co.

Reynolds, George W.M. (1849) *The Mysteries of the London Courts*, John Dickie

Sinclair, Iain (1995) *White Chappell Scarlet Tracings*, Vintage

Walford, Edward (1878) *Old and New London: Volume 6*, Cassell

Weeks, Margaret H. (1972) www.cryerfamilyhistory.co.uk/location-horsleydown.htm

Wilson, John Marius (1866) *Imperial Gazetteer of England and Wales*, A. Fullarton & Co.

4. THE LIBERTY OF NORTON FOLGATE

Burgess, Anthony (1994) *A Dead Man in Deptford*, Vintage

Burke, Thomas & Binder, Pearl (1932) *The Real East End*, Constable & Co. Ltd.

Greaves, Richard L. (1986) *Deliver Us From Evil: the Radical Underground in Britain 1660-1663*, Oxford University Press

The Gentle Author (2013) 'The Relics of Norton Folgate', 12th April 2013 spitalfieldslife.com/2013/04/12/the-relics-of-norton-folgate/ - accessed 13th April 2013

Hilton, Della (1977) *Who Was Kit Marlowe?* Taplinger Publishing Company

Journal of the House of Lords volume 31: 1765-1767 (1767-1830), History of Parliament Trust

Litvinoff, Emanuel (2008) 'A Jew in England', *Journey Through A Small Planet*, Penguin

London, Jack (1903, 2007) *People of the Abyss*, The Echo Library

Maddocks, Sydney (1932) 'Spitalfields' in *The Copartnership Herald*, Vol. II, no. 13 (March 1932)

Middleton, Thomas (2007) 'The Nightingale and the Ant', *The Collected Works*, Oxford University Press

Morrison, Arthur (1896) *A Child of the Jago*, Methuen & Co.

Pepys, Samuel (1669) *The Diary of Samuel Pepys* Vol. 9. University of California Press 2000

Pevsner, Nikolaus & Cherry, Bridget (1998) *The Buildings of England, London 4: North*, Penguin

Pevsner, Nikolaus, Cherry, Bridget & O'Brien, Charles (2005) *The Buildings of England, London 5: East*, Penguin

Shaw, George Bernard (1898) 'Candida', *Plays Pleasant*, Penguin Classics 2003

Sheppard, F.H.W. (1957) *Survey of London: Volume 27: Spitalfields and Mile End New Town*, Athlone Press for the London County Council

Stow, John (1598) *The Survey of London*, Everyman 1912

Strype, John (1720) *A Survey of the Cities of London and Westminster*

Wraight, A.D. (1994) *The Story That the Sonnets Tell*, Adam Hart

Zangwill, Israel (1893) *Children of the Ghetto*, W. Heinemann

5. LIMEHOUSE: LONDONS' FIRST CHINATOWN

Anon. (1868) 'East London Opium Smokers' in *London Society*, July 1868

Armfelt, Count E. (1902) 'Oriental London' in G.R. Sims (ed.) *Living London: Its Work and Its Play, Its Humour and Its Pathos, Its Sights and Its Scenes*, Vol. 2 Cassell and Company

Birch, J.G. (1930) *Limehouse Through Five Centuries,* The Sheldon Press

Berridge, Virginia and Edwards, Griffith (1981) *Opium and the People,* Lane

Burke, Thomas (1917) *Limehouse Nights: Tales of Chinatown*, Grant Richards

Burrows, Jon (2009) 'A Vague Chinese Quarter Elsewhere: Limehouse in the Cinema 1914-36' in *Journal of British Cinema and Television*, Vol. 6

Chung, Simone Shu-Yen (2008) 'The study of Chinatown as an urban artifice and its impact on the Chinese community in London.' Master's Thesis, University College London

Dickens, Charles (1870, 1973), *The Mystery of Edwin Drood*, Penguin

Dickens, Charles (the Younger) (1888), *Dickens' Dictionary of London*

www.victorianlondon.org/publications/dictionary.htm

Farson, Daniel (1991) *Limehouse Days*, Michael Joseph

Gilman, Sander L. and Xun, Zhou (2004) *Smoke: a Global History of Smoking*, Reaktion Books

Grange, Richard (2011) 'The Mixed-Race Families of Limehouse – Myth and Reality', *Mixed Britannia*, BBC

Hobhouse, Hermione (ed.) (1994) *Survey of London: volumes 43 and 44: Poplar, Blackwall and Isle of Dogs, English Heritage*

Irwin, Robert (2011) 'How and why the West misrepresents the East', *Times Literary Supplement*, 19th August 2011

Nairn, Ian (1966) *Nairn's London*, Penguin

Ng, Kwee Choo (1968) *The Chinese in London,* published for the Institute of Race Relations by Oxford University Press

Rohmer, Sax (2012) *The Mystery of Dr. Fu-Manchu*, Titan Books

Pevsner, Nikolaus, Cherry, Bridget & O'Brien, Charles (2005) *The Buildings of England, London 5: East*, Penguin

Pevsner, Nikolaus & Williamson, Elizabeth (1998) *The Buildings of England: London Docklands, An Architectural Guide*, Penguin

Seed, Dr. John (2010) 'The Chinese in Limehouse 1900-1940', 8th March 2010, untoldlondon.com

Seton Merriman, Henry (1902, 2006) *The Vultures*, The Echo Library

Shiel, M. P. (1898) *The Yellow Danger*, Grant Richards

Sims, George R. (1911) *Off the Track in London,* Jarrold & Sons

Tchen, John Kuo Wei (2012), 'The Yellow Claw: the Optical Unconscious in Anglo-American Political Culture', in Bold, Christine (ed.) *The Oxford History of Popular Print Culture Volume 6: US Popular Print Culture 1860-1920*, Oxford University Press

Tuchman, Barbara W. (1966) *The Proud Tower: A Portrait of the World Before the War 1890-1914,* Hamish Hamilton

Van Ash, Cay and Sax Rohmer, Elizabeth (1972) *Master of Villainy: A Biography of Sax Rohmer*, Tom Stacey

Witchard, Anne (2009) *Thomas Burke's Dark Chinoiserie*, Ashgate

6. OLD ST. PANCRAS

Beames, Thomas (1852) *The Rookeries of London*, Thomas Bosworth

Bradley, Simon (2007) *St. Pancras Station*, Profile Books

Brown, Jane, (1946) *I Had a Pitch on the Stones (Story of My Twenty Years in the Caledonian Market),* Nicholson & Watson

Chambers, R. (1869) *The Book of Days*, W & R Chambers

Coates, Chris (2001) *Utopia Britannica*, Diggers and Dreamers

Denford, Steven L.J. (1995) *Agar Town: The life and death of a Victorian "slum",* Camden History Society

Dun, Aidan Andrew (2010) *Vale Royal*, Dark Star

Dyos, H.J. (1955) "Railways and Housing in Victorian London" *Journal of Transport History*, Vol. 2, No.1, May 1955

Edwards, Marjorie (1989) *Up the Cally: the history and recollections of London's Old Caledonian Market*, Marketprompt

Goldsmith, Oliver (1762), *The Citizen of the World*, Perth: R. Morison and Son Ltd.

Hibbert, C. (1980, first published 1969) *London, The Biography of a City*, Penguin

Hollingshead, John (1861) *Ragged London in 1861*, Smith, Elder and Co.

Inwood, S. (1998) *A History of London*, Macmillan

Lovell, Percy and Marcham, William McB. (1938) *Survey of London: Volume 19*, London County Council

Morrell, Roger Conyers (1935) *The Story of Agar Town the ecclesiastical parish of St. Thomas' Camden Town*, The Author

Norden, John (1593) *Speculum Britanniae,* Johannes Norden

Porter, Roy (1994) *London: A Social History*, Penguin

Smith, James and Smith, Horace (1812) *Rejected Addresses or the New Theatrum Poetarum*, John Miller

Swensen, Steven P. (2006) Working Papers on the Nature of Evidence:

How Well Do 'Facts' Travel? No.09/06 "Mapping Poverty in Agar Town: Economic Conditions Prior to the Development of St. Pancras Station In 1866", London School of Economics

Swift, Jonathan (1996, originally published 1704) *A Tale of a Tub and other works*, Oxford University Press

Thomas, W.M. (1851) 'A Suburban Connemara', *Household Words*, 8th March 1851

Tindall, Gillian (1977), *The Fields Beneath*, Temple Smith

Walford, Edward (1878) *Old and New London: Volume 5*, Cassell

Walford, Edward (1878) *Old and New London: Volume 6*, Cassell

Wates, Nick (1976) *The Battle for Tolmers Square*, Routledge & Kegan Paul

7. RATCLIFF: SAILOR TOWN

Anon. (1933) *A Pictorial and Descriptive Guide to London*, Ward, Lock & Co.

Anon. (1857) 'Down the Highway', *East London Observer No. 4* Saturday 10th October, 1857

Besant, Walter (1901) *East London*, Century Co.

Burke, Thomas (1928) *East of Mansion House*, Cassell

Céline, Louis-Ferdinand (1954) *Guignol's Band*, New Directions

De Quincey, Thomas (2006) *On Murder*, Oxford University Press

Dickens, Charles (1865) *Our Mutual Friend*, Oxford World Classics 2008

Dickens, Charles (the Younger) (1888) *Dickens' Dictionary of London*

Ewing Ritchie, J. (1857) *The Night Side of London*, William Tweedie

Greenwood, James (1882) *Mysteries of Modern London* www.victorianlondon.org/districts/tigerbay.htm

James, P.D. & Critchley, T.A. (1987) *The Mall and the Pear Tree*, Sphere

Maddocks, Sydney (1935) 'Ratcliff' in *The Copartnership Herald*, Vol. III, no. 26 (April 1933) and Vol. V, no. 58 (December 1935)

Nairn, Ian (1966) *Nairn's London*, Penguin

Pevsner, Nikolaus, Cherry, Bridget & O'Brien, Charles (2005) *The Buildings of England, London 5: East*, Penguin

Phillips, Watts (1855) *The Wild Tribes of London*, London

Sinclair, Iain (1995) *Lud Heat* and *Suicide Bridge*, Vintage

Stow, John (1598) *The Survey of London*, Everyman 1912

8. STREATHAM SPA

Anon. (1803) *The life of Samuel Matthews, the Norwood Hermit*, Harrild & Billing

Arnold, F. (1886) *History of Streatham*, Elliot Stock

Baldwin, Herbert (1993) *Streatham Old and New*, Local History Reprints

Boswell, James (1791, 2008) *The Life of Samuel Johnson*, Penguin

Brown, John W. (1989) *Aubrey's History of Streatham*, Local History Reprints

Brown, John W. (1993) *Sherlock Holmes in Streatham*, Local History Publications

Brown, John W. (1999) *Streatham: Images of England*, Tempus Publishing Ltd.

Brown, John W., Brewer, Roger A., Davis, Cecil T. (2007) *A Chronology of the Parish of Streatham*, Local History Publications

Bryant, Kenneth (1998) *Streatham's 41*, The Streatham Society

Conan Doyle, Sir Arthur (1892) *The Adventures of Sherlock Holmes*, Penguin 2007

Farington, Joseph (1923) *The Farington Diary Vol.1 (July 13 1793 to August 24 1802)*, Hutchinson & Co.

Foord, A.S. (1910) *Springs, Streams and Spas of London*, T. Fisher Unwin

Gower, Graham (1996) *A History of Suburban Streatham*, Local History Publications

Grant, Lt.-Co.l F. (1887) *The Life of Dr Johnson*, Walter Scott, London

Pepys, Samuel (1669) *The Diary of Samuel Pepys* Vol. 9. University of California Press 2000

Pevsner, Nikolaus & Cherry, Bridget (2002) *The Buildings of England, London 2: South*, Penguin

Piozzi, Hester Lynch (1942) *Thraliana*, Balderston, Katherine C. (ed.) Clarendon Press, Oxford

Saward, Arthur A. (1907) *Reminiscences of Norwood* (copy in Minet Public Library).

Sexby, Lt.-Col. J. J. (1905) *History of Streatham Common*, Local History Reprints, 1991

Stevens Curl, James (2010) *Spas, Wells and Pleasure Gardens of London*, Historical Publications

White, Jerry (2012) *London in the Eighteenth Century*, Bodley Head

9. WELLCLOSE: THE FORGOTTEN EAST END

Anon. (undated) *History of the Parish, St.George-in-the-East*. stgite.org.uk accessed October 2012

Bergquist, Lars (2005) *Swedenborg's Secret*, The Swedenborg Society

Coverley, Merlin (2008) *Occult London*, Pocket Essentials

Defoe, Daniel (1978) *A Tour Through the Whole Island of Great Britain*, Penguin

Dickens, Charles (1868) 'Last of Old Stories Retold: The Accident at the Brunswick Theatre' *All the Year Round. Volume XX.* 13th June - 28th November, 1868

Glinert, Ed (2003) *East End Chronicles*, Penguin

Greenwood, James (1874) *The Wilds of London*, Guildford

Haymes, Alan (2010) *History of Ship Alley and Princes Square, Stepney, East London*, haimovitch.co.uk

Jamrach, Charles (1879) "My Struggle With a Tiger" in *The Boy's Own Paper*, Vol. I, no. 3 (1st February 1879)

Maddocks, Sydney (1934) "Well Close, Part One", in *The Copartnership Herald*, Vol. IV, No. 38, April 1934

McKie, Jean (2009) "Alphons Elder, Street Musician" www.jeaned.net/AlphonsEderBookrevised2009.pdf (accessed October 2012)

Nairn, Ian (1966) *Nairn's London*, Penguin

Pevsner, Nikolaus, Cherry, Bridget & O'Brien, Charles (2005) *The Buildings of England, London 5: East*, Penguin

Sims, George R. (1911) *Off the track in London*, Jarrold & Sons

Sinclair, Iain (1995) *Radon Daughters*, Vintage

Wilde, Oscar (1992) *The Picture of Dorian Gray*, Wordsworth Classics

Zangwill, Israel (1907) *Ghetto Comedies*, Heinemann

Williams, Frederick Benton (1897) *On Many Seas: the Life and Exploits of a Yankee Sailor*, The Macmillan Company

10. WHITE CITY: THE FIRST OLYMPIC PARK

Bowen, Elizabeth (1945) *To The North*, Penguin

Davey, Richard (1910) *The Tower of London*, EP Dutton & Co.

Hobhouse, Hermione (ed.) (1986) *Survey of London: Volume 42, Kensington Square to Earl's Court*, English Heritage

Girginov, Vassil (ed.) (2013) *Handbook of the London 2012 Olympic and Paralympic Games, Volume One: Making the Games*, Routledge

Glinert, Ed (2004) *The London Compendium*, Penguin

Kimber, Jane and Wheeldon, Anne (2005) *Images of London: Shepherd's Bush and White City*, Tempus

Knight, Donald R. (1978) *The Exhibitions: Great White City, Shepherds Bush London*, Barnard & Westwood Ltd.

Newland, Courttia (2001) *The Scholar*, Abacus

Royle, Nicholas (2000) *The Director's Cut*, Abacus

Sinclair, Iain (2012) *Ghost Milk: Calling Time on the Grand Project*, Hamish Hamilton

Sinclair, Iain (2004) *London Orbital: a Walk Around the M25*, Penguin

Sinclair, Iain (ed.) (2006) *London: City of Disappearances*, Hamish Hamilton

Westerby, Robert (1937), *Wide Boys Never Work*, John Lehmann

Willis, Ted (1950), *The Blue Lamp*, Convoy Publications Ltd.

Wise, Sarah (1998) 'Built Not to Last', *The Guardian*, 10th April 1998

ABOUT THE AUTHOR
Tom Bolton is the author of *London's Lost Rivers: A Walker's Guide* (Strange Attractor Press 2011). He is an urban writer and researcher, and also writes on music and theatre. Tom gives London talks and leads walks.

ABOUT THE PHOTOGRAPHS
These photographs were made with a Speed Graphic: a large format box camera first produced in 1912, and once the most famous press camera in the world. The particular model we used dates from the 1940s. The photographs were shot onto 4x5 Polaroid instant positive sheet film, which was first manufactured in 1958, but is no longer in production. We used the last available batch of Type 59, which has already long expired. It felt appropriate to use these beautiful but now archaic technologies to search for traces of a vanished city.
SF Said

ACKNOWLEDGEMENTS
For Jo.
Many thanks to:
Mark Pilkington for showing this book the light of day.
SF Said for photographing the vanished.
Peter and Rosalind Bolton for reading, commenting and editing.
Richard Bancroft for proofing the results.

SF Said would like to thank Rommel Pecson for the Speed Graphic camera, and for the inspiration.

Strange Attractor Press 2014